westermann

AF870657

EinFach Englisch

LITERATURE

Series Editor:
Iris Edelbrock

George Orwell

Animal Farm

Edited by
Kathrin Auer

Sprachliche Betreuung: John Poziemski

Druck A[2] / Jahr 2025
Alle Drucke der Serie A sind im Unterricht parallel verwendbar.

Redaktion: Marion Kramer
Umschlaggestaltung: LIO Design, Braunschweig; Foto: Alamy Stock Photo/Avalon/Photoshot License
Druck und Bindung: Westermann Druck GmbH, Georg-Westermann-Allee 66, 38104 Braunschweig

ISBN 978-3-14-**127472**-1

Contents

George Orwell
Animal Farm

Additional material

Additional texts

Skills & vocabulary

Chapter I

pop-hole hole for the chickens to go through
to lurch to stumble
barrel large wooden container
scullery *Waschküche*
to snore to make loud breathing noises while asleep
fluttering light and quick movement
boar [bɔːr] male pig
to exhibit to present in a show
to regard sb. highly to think the best of sb.
to be ensconced [ɪnˈskɒns] to sit comfortably
stout fat
benevolent [bəˈnevələnt] kind-hearted
tush tusk, a long pointed tooth
after their different fashions in their own unique ways
to perch [pɜːtʃ] to sit on the edge of sth.
rafter beam
to chew the cud *wiederkäuen*
vast very big
to conceal [kənˈsiːl] to hide
mare female horse
foal baby horse
hand unit for measuring the height of a horse, 10.2 cm
tremendous huge, very great, amazing
worst tempered the angriest

Mr Jones, of the Manor Farm, had locked the henhouses for the night, but was too drunk to remember to shut the pop-holes. With the ring of light from his lantern dancing from side to side, he lurched across the yard, kicked off his boots at the back door, drew himself a last glass of beer from the barrel in the scullery, and made his way up to bed, where Mrs Jones was already snoring.

As soon as the light in the bedroom went out there was a stirring and a fluttering all through the farm buildings. Word had gone round during the day that old Major, the prize Middle White boar, had had a strange dream on the previous night and wished to communicate it to the other animals. It had been agreed that they should all meet in the big barn as soon as Mr Jones was safely out of the way. Old Major (so he was always called, though the name under which he had been exhibited was Willingdon Beauty) was so highly regarded on the farm that everyone was quite ready to lose an hour's sleep in order to hear what he had to say.

At one end of the big barn, on a sort of raised platform, Major was already ensconced on his bed of straw, under a lantern which hung from a beam. He was twelve years old and had lately grown rather stout, but he was still a majestic-looking pig, with a wise and benevolent appearance in spite of the fact that his tushes had never been cut. Before long the other animals began to arrive and make themselves comfortable after their different fashions. First came the three dogs, Bluebell, Jessie and Pincher, and then the pigs, who settled down in the straw immediately in front of the platform. The hens perched themselves on the window-sills, the pigeons fluttered up to the rafters, the sheep and cows lay down behind the pigs and began to chew the cud. The two cart-horses, Boxer and Clover, came in together, walking very slowly and setting down their vast hairy hoofs with great care lest there should be some small animal concealed in the straw. Clover was a stout motherly mare approaching middle life, who had never quite got her figure back after her fourth foal. Boxer was an enormous beast, nearly eighteen hands high, and as strong as any two ordinary horses put together. A white stripe down his nose gave him a somewhat stupid appearance, and in fact he was not of first-rate intelligence, but he was universally respected for his steadiness of character and tremendous powers of work. After the horses came Muriel, the white goat, and Benjamin, the donkey. Benjamin was the oldest animal on the farm, and the worst tempered. He seldom talked, and when he did, it was usually to make some cynical remark – for instance, he would say that God had given him a tail to keep the flies off, but that he would sooner have had no tail and no flies. Alone among the animals on the farm he never laughed. If asked why, he would say that he saw nothing to laugh at. Nevertheless, without openly admitting it, he was devoted to Boxer; the two of them usually spent their Sundays together in the small paddock beyond the orchard, grazing side by side and never speaking.

The two horses had just lain down when a brood of ducklings, which had lost their mother, filed into the barn, cheeping feebly and wandering from side to side to find some place where they would not be trodden on. Clover made a sort of wall round them with her great foreleg, and the ducklings nestled down inside it and promptly fell asleep. At the last moment Mollie, the foolish, pretty white mare who drew Mr Jones's trap, came mincing daintily in, chewing at a lump of sugar. She took a place near the front and began flirting her white mane, hoping to draw attention to the red ribbons it was plaited with. Last of all came the cat, who looked round, as usual, for the warmest place, and finally squeezed herself in between Boxer and Clover; there she purred contentedly throughout Major's speech without listening to a word of what he was saying.

All the animals were now present except Moses, the tame raven, who slept on a perch behind the back door. When Major saw that they had all made themselves comfortable and were waiting attentively, he cleared his throat and began:

"Comrades, you have heard already about the strange dream that I had last night. But I will come to the dream later. I have something else to say first. I do not think, comrades, that I shall be with you for many months longer, and before I die, I feel it my duty to pass on to you such wisdom as I have acquired. I have had a long life, I have had much time for thought as I lay alone in my stall, and I think I may say that I understand the nature of life on this earth as well as any animal now living. It is about this that I wish to speak to you.

"Now, comrades, what is the nature of this life of ours? Let us face it: our lives are miserable, laborious and short. We are born, we are given just so much food as will keep the breath in our bodies, and those of us who are capable of it are forced to work to the last atom of our strength; and the very instant that our usefulness has come to an end we are slaughtered with hideous cruelty. No animal in England knows the meaning of happiness or leisure after he is a year old. No animal in England is free. The life of an animal is misery and slavery: that is the plain truth.

to admit to accept sth. to be true
devoted loyal
paddock small field where horses are kept
orchard [ˈɔːtʃəd] garden of fruit trees
to graze to eat grass
brood *Brut*
to cheep *piepsen*
feeble soft
to file walk in a row
to be trodden on to be trampled on

trap carriage
to mince daintily *(ironical)* to move delicately; *trippeln*
lump piece
to flirt *here*: to show off
mane horse's hair
plaited *geflochten*

contented satisfied

tame not wild; *zahm*
perch *Stange*

comrade (*old use*) *Genosse*

laborious requiring a lot of work

to slaughter to kill an animal to use its meat
hideous extremely horrific
leisure [ˈleʒər] free time

to dwell upon (dwelt, dwelt) to live in
soil the ground that plants grow in
abundance more than enough
dignity respect; *Würde*
root cause main reason
to abolish to end
plough *Pflug*
to till *beackern*
dung *Mist*
bare naked
sturdy strong and healthy
to hatch *here*: develop
confinement *(old use)* birth
rations fixed amount of food
to grumble to complain
porker *Mastschwein*
block slaughter block
fate the (bad) things that happen to you; *Schicksal*

"But is this simply part of the order of nature? Is it because this land of ours is so poor that it cannot afford a decent life to those who dwell upon it? No, comrades, a thousand times no! The soil of England is fertile, its climate is good, it is capable of affording food in abundance to an enormously greater number of animals than now inhabit it. This single farm of ours would support a dozen horses, twenty cows, hundreds of sheep – and all of them living in a comfort and a dignity that are now almost beyond our imagining. Why then do we continue in this miserable condition? Because nearly the whole of the produce of our labour is stolen from us by human beings. There, comrades, is the answer to all our problems. It is summed up in a single word – Man. Man is the only real enemy we have. Remove Man from the scene, and the root cause of hunger and overwork is abolished for ever.

"Man is the only creature that consumes without producing. He does not give milk, he does not lay eggs, he is too weak to pull the plough, he cannot run fast enough to catch rabbits. Yet he is lord of all the animals. He sets them to work, he gives back to them the bare minimum that will prevent them from starving, and the rest he keeps for himself. Our labour tills the soil, our dung fertilizes it, and yet there is not one of us that owns more than his bare skin. You cows that I see before me, how many thousands of gallons of milk have you given during this last year? And what has happened to that milk which should have been breeding up sturdy calves? Every drop of it has gone down the throats of our enemies. And you hens, how many eggs have you laid in this last year, and how many of those eggs ever hatched into chickens? The rest have all gone to market to bring in money for Jones and his men. And you, Clover, where are those four foals you bore, who should have been the support and pleasure of your old age? Each was sold at a year old – you will never see one of them again. In return for your four confinements and all your labour in the fields, what have you ever had except your bare rations and a stall?

"And even the miserable lives we lead are not allowed to reach their natural span. For myself I do not grumble, for I am one of the lucky ones. I am twelve years old and have had over four hundred children. Such is the natural life of a pig. But no animal escapes the cruel knife in the end. You young porkers who are sitting in front of me, every one of you will scream your lives out at the block within a year. To that horror we all must come – cows, pigs, hens, sheep, everyone. Even the horses and the dogs have no better fate. You, Boxer, the very day that those great muscles of yours lose their power, Jones will sell you to the knacker, who will cut your throat and boil you down for the fox-hounds. As for the dogs, when they grow old and toothless, Jones ties a brick round their necks and drowns them in the nearest pond.

"Is it not crystal clear, then, comrades, that all the evils of this life of ours spring from the tyranny of human beings? Only get rid of Man, and the produce of our labour would be our own. Almost overnight we could become rich and free. What then must we do? Why, work night and day, body and soul, for the overthrow of the human race! That is my message to you, comrades: Rebellion! I do not know when that Rebellion will come, it might be in a week or in a hundred years, but I know, as surely as I see this straw beneath my feet, that sooner or later justice will be done. Fix your eyes on that, comrades, throughout the short remainder of your lives! And above all, pass on this message of mine to those who come after you, so that future generations shall carry on the struggle until it is victorious.

"And remember, comrades, your resolution must never falter. No argument must lead you astray. Never listen when they tell you that Man and the animals have a common interest, that the prosperity of the one is the prosperity of the others. It is all lies. Man serves the interests of no creature except himself. And among us animals let there be perfect unity, perfect comradeship in the struggle. All men are enemies. All animals are comrades."

At this moment there was a tremendous uproar. While Major was speaking four large rats had crept out of their holes and were sitting on their hindquarters, listening to him. The dogs had suddenly caught sight of them, and it was only by a swift dash for their holes that the rats saved their lives. Major raised his trotter for silence.

"Comrades," he said, "here is a point that must be settled. The wild creatures, such as rats and rabbits – are they our friends or our enemies? Let us put it to the vote. I propose this question to the meeting: Are rats comrades?"

The vote was taken at once, and it was agreed by an overwhelming majority that rats were comrades. There were only four dissentients, the three dogs and the cat, who was afterwards discovered to have voted on both sides. Major continued:

"I have little more to say. I merely repeat, remember always your duty of enmity towards Man and all his ways. Whatever goes upon two legs is an enemy. Whatever goes upon four legs, or has wings, is a friend. And remember also that in fighting against Man, we must not come to resemble him. Even when you have conquered him, do not adopt his vices. No animal must ever live in a house, or sleep in a bed, or wear clothes, or drink alcohol, or

knacker *Abdecker*

pond small lake

to falter to become weak

to lead astray to direct away from the right path

prosperity (financial) well-being

uproar loud noise from protest

hindquarters *Hinterteil*

swift fast

dash run

trotter pig's foot

to propose to offer, to suggest

dissentient sb. whose opinion differs from the majority's

to resemble to be like

to conquer to overcome

vice negative trait; *Laster*

smoke tobacco, or touch money, or engage in trade. All the habits of Man are evil. And, above all, no animal must ever tyrannize over his own kind. Weak or strong, clever or simple, we are all brothers. No animal must ever kill any other animal. All animals are equal.

"And now, comrades, I will tell you about my dream of last night. I cannot describe that dream to you. It was a dream of the earth as it will be when Man has vanished. But it reminded me of something that I had long forgotten. Many years ago, when I was a little pig, my mother and the other sows used to sing an old song of which they knew only the tune and the first three words. I had known that tune in my infancy, but it had long since passed out of my mind. Last night, however, it came back to me in my dream. And what is more, the words of the song also came back – words, I am certain, which were sung by the animals of long ago and have been lost to memory for generations. I will sing you that song now, comrades. I am old and my voice is hoarse, but when I have taught you the tune, you can sing it better for yourselves. It is called 'Beasts of England'."

Old Major cleared his throat and began to sing. As he said, his voice was hoarse, but he sang well enough, and it was a stirring tune, something between 'Clementine' and 'La Cucuracha'. The words ran:

Beasts of England, beasts of Ireland,
Beasts of every land and clime,
Hearken to my joyful tidings
Of the golden future time.

Soon or late the day is coming,
Tyrant Man shall be o'erthrown,
And the fruitful fields of England
Shall be trod by beasts alone.

Rings shall vanish from our noses,
And the harness from our back,
Bit and spur shall rust forever,
Cruel whips no more shall crack.

Riches more than mind can picture,
Wheat and barley, oats and hay,
Clover, beans and mangel-wurzels
Shall be ours upon that day.

to vanish to disappear
tune melody
infancy early childhood
hoarse rough
stirring moving
clime (*old use*) climate
to hearken *(old use)* to listen
tidings *(fml., old use)* news
to be trod (*past participle of tread*) to be walked on
harness *Geschirr*
bit and spur *Trense und Sporen*
whip long piece of leather used to beat animals
wheat and barley *Weizen und Gerste*
clover *Klee*
mangel-wurzel *Zuckerrübe*

Bright will shine the fields of England,
Purer shall its waters be,
Sweeter yet shall blow its breezes
On the day that sets us free.

For that day we all must labour,
Though we die before it break;
Cows and horses, geese and turkeys,
All must toil for freedom's sake.

Beasts of England, beasts of Ireland,
Beasts of every land and clime,
Hearken well and spread my tidings
Of the golden future time.

The singing of this song threw the animals into the wildest excitement. Almost before Major had reached the end, they had begun singing it for themselves. Even the stupidest of them had already picked up the tune and a few of the words, and as for the clever ones, such as the pigs and dogs, they had the entire song by heart within a few minutes. And then, after a few preliminary tries, the whole farm burst out into 'Beasts of England' in tremendous unison. The cows lowed it, the dogs whined it, the sheep bleated it, the horses whinnied it, the ducks quacked it. They were so delighted with the song that they sang it right through five times in succession, and might have continued singing it all night if they had not been interrupted.
Unfortunately, the uproar awoke Mr Jones, who sprang out of bed, making sure that there was a fox in the yard. He seized the gun which always stood in a corner of his bedroom, and let fly a charge of number 6 shot into the darkness. The pellets buried themselves in the wall of the barn and the meeting broke up hurriedly. Everyone fled to his own sleeping-place. The birds jumped on to their perches, the animals settled down in the straw, and the whole farm was asleep in a moment.

breeze light wind

to break (of a day) to begin

to toil to work hard, to struggle

preliminary [prɪˈlɪmɪnəri] first, preparatory

in unison at the same time, in harmony
to low *muhen*
to whine *winseln*
to bleat *blöcken*
to whinny *wiehern*
to quack *schnattern*

to seize [siːz] to grab

charge *Salve*
shot *Schrott(kugel)*
pellet small round metal ball shot from an air gun

Chapter II

foot *here*: furthest corner

pre-eminent (*fml.*) the best

vivacious [vɪˈveɪʃəs] active and lively

porker young pig

nimble light and quick

persuasive [pəˈsweɪsɪv] convincing

to elaborate to develop by adding detail

to expound [ɪkˈspaʊnd] to explain

contrary to against

Three nights later old Major died peacefully in his sleep. His body was buried at the foot of the orchard.

This was early in March. During the next three months there was much secret activity. Major's speech had given to the more intelligent animals on the farm a completely new outlook on life. They did not know when the Rebellion predicted by Major would take place, they had no reason for thinking that it would be within their own lifetime, but they saw clearly that it was their duty to prepare for it. The work of teaching and organizing the others fell naturally upon the pigs, who were generally recognized as being the cleverest of the animals. Pre-eminent among the pigs were two young boars named Snowball and Napoleon, whom Mr Jones was breeding up for sale. Napoleon was a large, rather fierce-looking Berkshire boar, the only Berkshire on the farm, not much of a talker, but with a reputation for getting his own way. Snowball was a more vivacious pig than Napoleon, quicker in speech and more inventive, but was not considered to have the same depth of character. All the other male pigs on the farm were porkers. The best known among them was a small pig named Squealer, with very round cheeks, twinkling eyes, nimble movements, and a shrill voice. He was a brilliant talker, and when he was arguing some difficult point he had a way of skipping from side to side and whisking his tail, which was somehow very persuasive. The others said of Squealer that he could turn black into white.

These three had elaborated old Major's teachings into a complete system of thought, to which they gave the name of Animalism. Several nights a week, after Mr Jones was asleep, they held secret meetings in the barn and expounded the principles of Animalism to the others. At the beginning they met with much stupidity and apathy. Some of the animals talked of the duty of loyalty to Mr Jones, whom they referred to as 'Master', or made elementary remarks such as "Mr Jones feeds us. If he were gone, we should starve to death." Others asked such questions as "Why should we care what happens after we are dead?" or "If this Rebellion is to happen anyway, what difference does it make whether we work for it or not?", and the pigs had great difficulty in making them see that this was contrary to the spirit of Animalism. The stupidest questions of all were asked by Mollie, the white mare. The very first question she asked Snowball was: "Will there still be sugar after the Rebellion?"

"No," said Snowball firmly. "We have no means of making sugar on this farm. Besides, you do not need sugar. You will have all the oats and hay you want."

"And shall I still be allowed to wear ribbons in my mane?" asked Mollie.

"Comrade," said Snowball, "those ribbons that you are so devoted to are the badge of slavery. Can you not understand that liberty is worth more than ribbons?"

Mollie agreed, but she did not sound very convinced.

The pigs had an even harder struggle to counteract the lies put about by Moses, the tame raven. Moses, who was Mr Jones's especial pet, was a spy and a talebearer, but he was also a clever talker. He claimed to know of the existence of a mysterious country called Sugarcandy Mountain, to which all animals went when they died. It was situated somewhere up in the sky, a little distance beyond the clouds, Moses said. In Sugarcandy Mountain it was Sunday seven days a week, clover was in season all the year round, and lump sugar and linseed cake grew on the hedges. The animals hated Moses because he told tales and did no work, but some of them believed in Sugarcandy Mountain, and the pigs had to argue very hard to persuade them that there was no such place.

Their most faithful disciples were the two carthorses, Boxer and Clover. These two had great difficulty in thinking anything out for themselves, but, having once accepted the pigs as their teachers, they absorbed everything that they were told, and passed it on to the other animals by simple arguments. They were unfailing in their attendance at the secret meetings in the barn, and led the singing of 'Beasts of England', with which the meetings always ended.

Now, as it turned out, the Rebellion was achieved much earlier and more easily than anyone had expected. In past years Mr Jones, although a hard master, had been a capable farmer, but of late he had fallen on evil days. He had become much disheartened after losing money in a lawsuit, and had taken to drinking more than was good for him. For whole days at a time he would lounge in his Windsor chair in the kitchen, reading the newspapers, drinking, and occasionally feeding Moses on crusts of bread soaked in beer. His men were idle and dishonest, the fields were full of weeds, the buildings wanted roofing, the hedges were neglected and the animals were underfed.

June came and the hay was almost ready for cutting. On Midsummer's Eve, which was a Saturday, Mr Jones went into Willingdon and got so drunk at the Red Lion that he did not come

ribbon *Schleife*

badge small piece of metal or plastic showing sb.'s rank or membership

to counteract to act against

talebearer sb. who gossips or lies about others

lump sugar *Zuckerklumpen*
linseed *Leinsamen*
hedge *Hecke*

disciple [dɪˈsaɪpəl] follower of a philosophy; *Jünger*

unfailing totally reliable

to be disheartened to lose motivation
lawsuit *Klage*

to lounge to sit comfortably
Windsor chair solid wooden chair

idle lazy

weeds unwanted plants; *Unkraut*
to want *here*: to need
to neglect to not care for sth.

back till midday on Sunday. The men had milked the cows in the early morning and then had gone out rabbiting, without bothering to feed the animals. When Mr Jones got back he immediately went to sleep on the drawing-room sofa with the *News of the World* over his face, so that, when evening came, the animals were still unfed. At last they could stand it no longer. One of the cows broke in the door of the store-shed with her horn and all the animals began to help themselves from the bins. It was just then that Mr Jones woke up. The next moment he and his four men were in the store-shed with whips in their hands, lashing out in all directions. This was more than the hungry animals could bear. With one accord, though nothing of the kind had been planned beforehand, they flung themselves upon their tormentors. Jones and his men suddenly found themselves being butted and kicked from all sides. The situation was quite out of their control. They had never seen animals behave like this before, and this sudden uprising of creatures whom they were used to thrashing and maltreating just as they chose, frightened them almost out of their wits. After only a moment or two they gave up trying to defend themselves and took to their heels. A minute later all five of them were in full flight down the cart-track that led to the main road, with the animals pursuing them in triumph.

Mrs Jones looked out of the bedroom window, saw what was happening, hurriedly flung a few possessions into a carpet bag, and slipped out of the farm by another way. Moses sprang off his perch and flapped after her, croaking loudly. Meanwhile the animals had chased Jones and his men out on to the road and slammed the five-barred gate behind them. And so, almost before they knew what was happening, the Rebellion had been successfully carried through: Jones was expelled, and the Manor Farm was theirs.

For the first few minutes the animals could hardly believe in their good fortune. Their first act was to gallop in a body right round the boundaries of the farm, as though to make quite sure that no human being was hiding anywhere upon it; then they raced back to the farm buildings to wipe out the last traces of Jones's hated reign. The harness-room at the end of the stables was broken open; the bits, the nose-rings, the dog-chains, the cruel knives with which Mr Jones had been used to castrate the pigs and lambs, were all flung down the well. The reins, the halters, the blinkers, the degrading nosebags, were thrown on to the rubbish fire which was burning in the yard. So were the whips. All the animals capered with joy when they saw the whips going up in flames. Snowball also threw on to the fire the ribbons with

to bother to care

drawing-room formal sitting room
News of the World British tabloid Sunday newspaper; closed in July 2011

to lash out to hit with great force

to bear to tolerate
with one accord (*fml.*) all together

tormentor (*fml.*) *Peiniger*

to butt to hit or push with the head or horns

uprising rebellion; *Aufstand*

to thrash to hit hard
to maltreat to treat badly
to frighten sb. out of their wits to scare sb. very much
to take to one's heels to flee, to run away
to pursue [pəˈsjuː] to run after

carpet bag *(old use) Reisetasche*

to expel to make sb. leave

good fortune luck
in a body all together
boundary borderline

reign rule

well *Brunnen*
reins *Zügel*
halter *Halfter*
blinkers *Scheuklappen*
degrading treating without respect
to caper (*fml.*) to jump around happily

which the horses' manes and tails had usually been decorated on market days.

"Ribbons," he said, "should be considered as clothes, which are the mark of a human being. All animals should go naked."

When Boxer heard this he fetched the small straw hat which he wore in summer to keep the flies out of his ears, and flung it on to the fire with the rest.

In a very little while the animals had destroyed everything that reminded them of Mr Jones. Napoleon then led them back to the store-shed and served out a double ration of corn to everybody, with two biscuits for each dog. Then they sang 'Beasts of England' from end to end seven times running, and after that they settled down for the night and slept as they had never slept before.

But they woke at dawn as usual, and suddenly remembering the glorious thing that had happened, they all raced out into the pasture together. A little way down the pasture there was a knoll that commanded a view of most of the farm. The animals rushed to the top of it and gazed round them in the clear morning light. Yes, it was theirs – everything that they could see was theirs! In the ecstasy of that thought they gambolled round and round, they hurled themselves into the air in great leaps of excitement. They rolled in the dew, they cropped mouthfuls of the sweet summer grass, they kicked up clods of the black earth and snuffed its rich scent. Then they made a tour of inspection of the whole farm and surveyed with speechless admiration the ploughland, the hayfield, the orchard, the pool, the spinney. It was as though they had never seen these things before, and even now they could hardly believe that it was all their own.

Then they filed back to the farm buildings and halted in silence outside the door of the farmhouse. That was theirs too, but they were frightened to go inside. After a moment, however, Snowball and Napoleon butted the door open with their shoulders and the animals entered in single file, walking with the utmost care for fear of disturbing anything. They tiptoed from room to room, afraid to speak above a whisper and gazing with a kind of awe at the unbelievable luxury, at the beds with their feather mattresses, the looking-glasses, the horsehair sofa, the Brussels carpet, the lithograph of Queen Victoria over the drawing-room mantelpiece. They were just coming down the stairs when Mollie was discovered to be missing. Going back, the others found that she had remained behind in the best bedroom. She had taken a piece of blue ribbon from Mrs Jones's dressing-table, and was holding it against her shoulder and admiring herself in the glass in a very foolish manner. The others reproached her sharply, and they

to fling (flung, flung) to throw

pasture [ˈpɑːstʃər] field of grass

knoll small hill

to gaze to look

to gambol to jump playfully

to hurl to throw

leap jump

dew [dʒuː] *Morgentau*

to crop to eat the tops of plants

clod lump

to snuff to smell, to breathe in

scent smell

to survey to examine to get an overview

spinney small group of trees

utmost biggest

to tiptoe to walk quietly on the tips of your feet

looking-glass (*old use*) mirror

mantelpiece *Kaminsims*

to reproach (*fml.*) to criticize

ham *Schinken*
scullery kitchen
to stave (stove, stove) *(old use)* to break
unanimous [juːˈnænɪməs] agreed upon by everyone
on the spot there and then

went outside. Some hams hanging in the kitchen were taken out for burial, and the barrel of beer in the scullery was stove in with a kick from Boxer's hoof, otherwise nothing in the house was touched. A unanimous resolution was passed on the spot that the farmhouse should be preserved as a museum. All were agreed that no animal must ever live there.

The animals had their breakfast, and then Snowball and Napoleon called them together again.

harvest *Ernte*
to attend to to pay attention to

"Comrades," said Snowball, "it is half-past six and we have a long day before us. Today we begin the hay harvest. But there is another matter that must be attended to first."

to give on to to lead to
knuckle [ˈnʌkəl] *Gelenk*

The pigs now revealed that during the past three months they had taught themselves to read and write from an old spelling book which had belonged to Mr Jones's children and which had been thrown on the rubbish heap. Napoleon sent for pots of black and white paint and led the way down to the five-barred gate that gave on to the main road. Then Snowball (for it was Snowball who was best at writing) took a brush between the two knuckles of his trotter, painted out Manor Farm from the top bar of the gate and in its place painted Animal Farm. This was to be the name of the farm from now onwards. After this they went back to the farm buildings, where Snowball and Napoleon sent for a ladder, which they caused to be set against the end wall of the big barn. They explained that by their studies of the past three months the pigs had succeeded in reducing the principles of Animalism to Seven Commandments. These Seven Commandments would now be inscribed on the wall; they would form an unalterable law by which all the animals on Animal Farm must live for ever after. With some difficulty (for it is not easy for a pig to balance himself on a ladder) Snowball climbed up and set to work, with Squealer a few rungs below him holding the paint-pot. The Commandments were written on the tarred wall in great white letters that could be read thirty yards away. They ran thus:

commandment order; *Gebot*
to inscribe to write on
unalterable *(fml.)* unchangeable
rung step on a ladder
tarred blackened by tar *(Teer)*

The Seven Commandments

1. *Whatever goes upon two legs is an enemy.*
2. *Whatever goes upon four legs, or has wings, is a friend.*
3. *No animal shall wear clothes.*
4. *No animal shall sleep in a bed.*
5. *No animal shall drink alcohol.*
6. *No animal shall kill any other animal.*
7. *All animals are equal.*

neatly well

It was very neatly written, and except that 'friend' was written 'freind' and one of the 'S's' was the wrong way round, the spelling was correct all the way through. Snowball read it aloud for the benefit of the others. All the animals nodded in complete agreement, and the cleverer ones at once began to learn the Commandments by heart.

"Now, comrades," cried Snowball, throwing down the paint-brush, "to the hayfield! Let us make it a point of honour to get in the harvest more quickly than Jones and his men could do."

But at this moment the three cows, who had seemed uneasy for some time past, set up a loud lowing. They had not been milked for twenty-four hours, and their udders were almost bursting. After a little thought, the pigs sent for buckets and milked the cows fairly successfully, their trotters being well adapted to this task. Soon there were five buckets of frothing creamy milk at which many of the animals looked with considerable interest.

"What is going to happen to all that milk?" said someone.

"Jones used sometimes to mix some of it in our mash," said one of the hens.

"Never mind the milk, comrades!" cried Napoleon, placing himself in front of the buckets. "That will be attended to. The harvest is more important. Comrade Snowball will lead the way. I shall follow in a few minutes. Forward, comrades! The hay is waiting."

So the animals trooped down to the hayfield to begin the harvest, and when they came back in the evening it was noticed that the milk had disappeared.

uneasy unsure, worried

udder *Euter*

to froth [frɒθ] to bubble

mash animal food mixture

to troop to go together in a group

Chapter III

How they toiled and sweated to get the hay in! But their efforts were rewarded, for the harvest was an even bigger success than they had hoped.

Sometimes the work was hard; the implements had been designed for human beings and not for animals, and it was a great drawback that no animal was able to use any tool that involved standing on his hind legs. But the pigs were so clever that they could think of a way round every difficulty. As for the horses, they knew every inch of the field, and in fact understood the business of mowing and raking far better than Jones and his men had ever done. The pigs did not actually work, but directed and supervised the others. With their superior knowledge it was natural that they should assume the leadership. Boxer and Clover would harness themselves to the cutter or the horse-rake (no bits or reins were needed in these days, of course) and tramp steadily round and round the field with a pig walking behind and calling out "Gee up, comrade!" or "Whoa back, comrade!" as the case might be. And every animal down to the humblest worked at turning the hay and gathering it. Even the ducks and hens toiled to and fro all day in the sun, carrying tiny wisps of hay in their beaks. In the end they finished the harvest in two days' less time than it had usually taken Jones and his men. Moreover, it was the biggest harvest that the farm had ever seen. There was no wastage whatever; the hens and ducks with their sharp eyes had gathered up the very last stalk. And not an animal on the farm had stolen so much as a mouthful.

All through that summer the work of the farm went like clockwork. The animals were happy as they had never conceived it possible to be. Every mouthful of food was an acute positive pleasure, now that it was truly their own food, produced by themselves and for themselves, not doled out to them by a grudging master. With the worthless parasitical human beings gone, there was more for everyone to eat. There was more leisure too, inexperienced though the animals were. They met with many difficulties – for instance, later in the year, when they harvested the corn, they had to tread it out in the ancient style and blow away the chaff with their breath, since the farm possessed no threshing machine – but the pigs with their cleverness and Boxer with his tremendous muscles always pulled them through. Boxer was the admiration of everybody. He had been a hard worker even in Jones's time, but now he seemed more like three horses than one; there were days when the entire work of the

implement tool
drawback disadvantage
hind leg back leg
to mow (mowed, mown) to cut grass
to rake *harken*
to direct to give orders
to supervise ['su:pəvaɪz] to watch over sb./sth.
superior better
to assume to take over
humblest lowest
to gather to collect
to and fro back and forth
wisp thin piece
beak a bird's mouth
wastage ['weɪstɪdʒ] waste
stalk *Stengel*
to conceive [kən'si:v] to believe, to imagine
to dole out (*infml.*) to hand out
grudging *widerwillig*
to tread sth. out to press sth. out with your feet
chaff dried grass used as animal food; *Spreu*
threshing machine *Dreschmaschine*

farm seemed to rest on his mighty shoulders. From morning to night he was pushing and pulling, always at the spot where the work was hardest. He had made an arrangement with one of the cockerels to call him in the mornings half an hour earlier than anyone else, and would put in some volunteer labour at whatever seemed to be most needed, before the regular day's work began. His answer to every problem, every setback, was "I will work harder!" – which he had adopted as his personal motto.

But everyone worked according to his capacity. The hens and ducks for instance, saved five bushels of corn at the harvest by gathering up the stray grains. Nobody stole, nobody grumbled over his rations, the quarrelling and biting and jealousy which had been normal features of life in the old days had almost disappeared. Nobody shirked – or almost nobody. Mollie, it was true, was not good at getting up in the mornings, and had a way of leaving work early on the ground that there was a stone in her hoof. And the behaviour of the cat was somewhat peculiar. It was soon noticed that when there was work to be done the cat could never be found. She would vanish for hours on end, and then reappear at mealtimes, or in the evening after work was over, as though nothing had happened. But she always made such excellent excuses, and purred so affectionately, that it was impossible not to believe in her good intentions. Old Benjamin, the donkey, seemed quite unchanged since the Rebellion. He did his work in the same slow obstinate way as he had done it in Jones's time, never shirking and never volunteering for extra work either. About the Rebellion and its results he would express no opinion. When asked whether he was not happier now that Jones was gone, he would say only "Donkeys live a long time. None of you has ever seen a dead donkey," and the others had to be content with this cryptic answer.

On Sundays there was no work. Breakfast was an hour later than usual, and after breakfast there was a ceremony which was observed every week without fail. First came the hoisting of the flag. Snowball had found in the harness-room an old green tablecloth of Mrs Jones's and had painted on it a hoof and a horn in white. This was run up the flagstaff in the farmhouse garden every Sunday morning. The flag was green, Snowball explained, to represent the green fields of England, while the hoof and horn signified the future Republic of the Animals which would arise when the human race had been finally overthrown. After the hoisting of the flag all the animals trooped into the big barn for a general assembly which was known as the Meeting. Here the work of the coming week was planned out and resolutions were put forward and debated. It was always the pigs who put for-

cockerel male chicken

volunteer doing sth. without being forced to

setback *Rückschlag*

bushel unit of measurement, just over 27 kg

to grumble to complain

stray single

to shirk to avoid work

peculiar unusual

to purr *schnurren*

affectionate caring, feeling

obstinate strong-willed

cryptic mysterious

to hoist to raise

flagstaff flagpole

assembly official meeting

to put forward a resolution to suggest a plan

ward the resolutions. The other animals understood how to vote, but could never think of any resolutions of their own. Snowball and Napoleon were by far the most active in the debates. But it was noticed that these two were never in agreement: whatever suggestion either of them made, the other could be counted on to oppose it. Even when it was resolved – a thing no one could object to in itself – to set aside the small paddock behind the orchard as a home of rest for animals who were past work, there was a stormy debate over the correct retiring age for each class of animal. The Meeting always ended with the singing of 'Beasts of England', and the afternoon was given up to recreation.

The pigs had set aside the harness-room as a headquarters for themselves. Here, in the evenings, they studied blacksmithing, carpentering, and other necessary arts from books which they had brought out of the farmhouse. Snowball also busied himself with organizing the other animals into what he called Animal Committees. He was indefatigable at this. He formed the Egg Production Committee for the hens, the Clean Tails League for the cows, the Wild Comrades' Re-education Committee (the object of this was to tame the rats and rabbits), the Whiter Wool Movement for the sheep, and various others, besides instituting classes in reading and writing. On the whole, these projects were a failure. The attempt to tame the wild creatures, for instance, broke down almost immediately. They continued to behave very much as before, and when treated with generosity, simply took advantage of it. The cat joined the Re-education Committee and was very active in it for some days. She was seen one day sitting on a roof and talking to some sparrows who were just out of her reach. She was telling them that all animals were now comrades and that any sparrow who chose could come and perch on her paw; but the sparrows kept their distance.

The reading and writing classes, however, were a great success. By the autumn almost every animal on the farm was literate in some degree.

As for the pigs, they could already read and write perfectly. The dogs learned to read fairly well, but were not interested in reading anything except the Seven Commandments. Muriel, the goat, could read somewhat better than the dogs, and sometimes used to read to the others in the evenings from scraps of newspaper which she found on the rubbish heap. Benjamin could read as well as any pig, but never exercised his faculty. So far as he knew, he said, there was nothing worth reading. Clover learnt the whole alphabet, but could not put words together. Boxer could not get beyond the letter D. He would trace out A, B, C, D in the dust with his great hoof, and then would stand staring at the let-

to resolve to solve a problem
to set aside to use
retiring age the age at which you stop working
recreation free-time activity
blacksmithing *Metallschmiederei*
carpentering *Zimmerei*
indefatigable [ˌɪndɪˈfætɪɡəbəl] (*fml.*) never getting tired
generosity *Großzügigkeit*
sparrow *Spatz*
paw *Pfote*
literate knowing how to read and write
faculty talent, ability

ters with his ears back, sometimes shaking his forelock, trying with all his might to remember what came next and never succeeding. On several occasions, indeed, he did learn E, F, G, H, but by the time he knew them, it was always discovered that he had forgotten A, B, C and D. Finally he decided to be content with the first four letters, and used to write them out once or twice every day to refresh his memory. Mollie refused to learn any but the six letters which spelt her own name. She would form these very neatly out of pieces of twig, and would then decorate them with a flower or two and walk round them admiring them.

None of the other animals on the farm could get further than the letter A. It was also found that the stupider animals, such as the sheep, hens and ducks, were unable to learn the Seven Commandments by heart. After much thought Snowball declared that the Seven Commandments could in effect be reduced to a single maxim, namely: 'Four legs good, two legs bad.' This, he said, contained the essential principle of Animalism. Whoever had thoroughly grasped it would be safe from human influences. The birds at first objected, since it seemed to them that they also had two legs, but Snowball proved to them that this was not so.

"A bird's wing, comrades," he said, "is an organ of propulsion and not of manipulation. It should therefore be regarded as a leg. The distinguishing mark of man is the *hand*, the instrument with which he does all his mischief."

The birds did not understand Snowball's long words, but they accepted his explanation, and all the humbler animals set to work to learn the new maxim by heart. Four Legs Good, Two Legs Bad was inscribed on the end wall of the barn, above the Seven Commandments and in bigger letters. When they had once got it by heart, the sheep developed a great liking for this maxim, and often as they lay in the field they would all start bleating 'Four legs good, two legs bad! Four legs good, two legs bad!' and keep it up for hours on end, never growing tired of it.

Napoleon took no interest in Snowball's committees. He said that the education of the young was more important than anything that could be done for those who were already grown up. It happened that Jessie and Bluebell had both whelped soon after the hay harvest, giving birth between them to nine sturdy puppies. As soon as they were weaned, Napoleon took them away from their mothers, saying that he would make himself responsible for their education. He took them up into a loft which could only be reached by a ladder from the harness-room, and there kept them in such seclusion that the rest of the farm soon forgot their existence.

The mystery of where the milk went to was soon cleared up. It was mixed every day into the pigs' mash. The early apples were

forelock *Stirnlocke*

maxim rule

thoroughly ['θʌrəli] completely
to grasp to understand
to object to disagree

propulsion a force that moves sth. forward

mischief ['mɪstʃɪf] bad or harmful behaviour

humbler *here*: less intelligent

to whelp to have puppies

to wean to stop breastfeeding

loft *Dachboden*
seclusion isolation

to litter to spread things, making a place look untidy
windfall *Fallobst*

now ripening, and the grass of the orchard was littered with windfalls. The animals had assumed as a matter of course that these would be shared out equally; one day, however, the order went forth that all the windfalls were to be collected and brought to the harness-room for the use of the pigs. At this some of the other animals murmured, but it was no use. All the pigs were in full agreement on this point, even Snowball and Napoleon. Squealer was sent to make the necessary explanations to the others.

to murmur [ˈmɜːmər] to complain in a low voice

"Comrades!" he cried. "You do not imagine, I hope, that we pigs are doing this in a spirit of selfishness and privilege? Many of us actually dislike milk and apples. I dislike them myself. Our sole object in taking these things is to preserve our health. Milk and apples (this has been proved by Science, comrades) contain substances absolutely necessary to the well-being of a pig. We pigs are brainworkers. The whole management and organization of this farm depend on us. Day and night we are watching over your welfare. It is for your sake that we drink that milk and eat those apples. Do you know what would happen if we pigs failed in our duty? Jones would come back! Yes, Jones would come back! Surely, comrades," cried Squealer almost pleadingly, skipping from side to side and whisking his tail, "surely there is no one among you who wants to see Jones come back?"

to plead to ask strongly for support

Now if there was one thing that the animals were completely certain of, it was that they did not want Jones back. When it was put to them in this light, they had no more to say. The importance of keeping the pigs in good health was all too obvious. So it was agreed without further argument that the milk and the windfall apples (and also the main crop of apples when they ripened) should be reserved for the pigs alone.

crop *Ernte*

Chapter IV

By the late summer the news of what had happened on Animal Farm had spread across half the county. Every day Snowball and Napoleon sent out flights of pigeons whose instructions were to mingle with the animals on neighbouring farms, tell them the story of the Rebellion, and teach them the tune of 'Beasts of England'.

to mingle to mix

Most of this time Mr Jones had spent sitting in the taproom of the Red Lion at Willingdon, complaining to anyone who would listen of the monstrous injustice he had suffered in being turned out of his property by a pack of good-for-nothing animals. The other farmers sympathized in principle, but they did not at first give him much help. At heart, each of them was secretly wondering whether he could not somehow turn Jones's misfortune to his own advantage. It was lucky that the owners of the two farms which adjoined Animal Farm were on permanently bad terms. One of them, which was named Foxwood, was a large, neglected, old-fashioned farm, much overgrown by woodland, with all its pastures worn out and its hedges in a disgraceful condition. Its owner, Mr Pilkington, was an easy-going gentleman farmer who spent most of his time in fishing or hunting according to the season. The other farm, which was called Pinchfield, was smaller and better kept. Its owner was a Mr Frederick, a tough shrewd man, perpetually involved in lawsuits and with a name for driving hard bargains. These two disliked each other so much that it was difficult for them to come to any agreement, even in defence of their own interests.

taproom bar

to adjoin to be next to

disgraceful shockingly bad

gentleman farmer sb. who owns a farm but has a manager to run it

shrewd [ʃru:d] clever and calculating

perpetual constant

to drive a hard bargain (drove, driven) to make no compromises when doing business

Nevertheless, they were both thoroughly frightened by the rebellion on Animal Farm, and very anxious to prevent their own animals from learning too much about it. At first they pretended to laugh to scorn the idea of animals managing a farm for themselves. The whole thing would be over in a fortnight, they said. They put it about that the animals on the Manor Farm (they insisted on calling it the Manor Farm; they would not tolerate the name 'Animal Farm') were perpetually fighting among themselves and were also rapidly starving to death. When time passed and the animals had evidently not starved to death, Frederick and Pilkington changed their tune and began to talk of the terrible wickedness that now flourished on Animal Farm. It was given out that the animals there practised cannibalism, tortured one another with red-hot horseshoes, and had their females in common. This was what came of rebelling against the laws of Nature, Frederick and Pilkington said.

to scorn [skɔ:n] to make fun of

fortnight two weeks

to put it about to spread the news

to pass to go by

wickedness evil

to flourish ['flʌrɪʃ] to develop

to have in common to share

However, these stories were never fully believed. Rumours of a wonderful farm, where the human beings had been turned out and the animals managed their own affairs, continued to circulate in vague and distorted forms, and throughout that year a wave of rebelliousness ran through the countryside. Bulls which had always been tractable suddenly turned savage, sheep broke down hedges and devoured the clover, cows kicked the pail over, hunters refused their fences and shot their riders on to the other side. Above all, the tune and even the words of 'Beasts of England' were known everywhere. It had spread with astonishing speed. The human beings could not contain their rage when they heard this song, though they pretended to think it merely ridiculous. They could not understand, they said, how even animals could bring themselves to sing such contemptible rubbish. Any animal caught singing it was given a flogging on the spot. And yet the song was irrepressible. The blackbirds whistled it in the hedges, the pigeons cooed it in the elms, it got into the din of the smithies and the tune of the church bells. And when the human beings listened to it, they secretly trembled, hearing in it a prophecy of their future doom.

Early in October, when the corn was cut and stacked and some of it was already threshed, a flight of pigeons came whirling through the air and alighted in the yard of Animal Farm in the wildest excitement. Jones and all his men, with half a dozen others from Foxwood and Pinchfield, had entered the five-barred gate and were coming up the cart-track that led to the farm. They were all carrying sticks, except Jones, who was marching ahead with a gun in his hands. Obviously they were going to attempt the recapture of the farm.

This had long been expected, and all preparations had been made. Snowball, who had studied an old book of Julius Caesar's campaigns which he had found in the farmhouse, was in charge of the defensive operations. He gave his orders quickly, and in a couple of minutes every animal was at his post.

As the human beings approached the farm buildings, Snowball launched his first attack. All the pigeons, to the number of thirty-five flew to and fro over the men's heads and dropped their dung on them from mid-air; and while the men were dealing with this, the geese, who had been hiding behind the hedge, rushed out and pecked viciously at the calves of their legs. However, this was only a light skirmishing manoeuvre, intended to create a little disorder, and the men easily drove the geese off with their sticks. Snowball now launched his second line of attack. Muriel, Benjamin, and all the sheep, with Snowball at the head of them, rushed forward and prodded and butted the men from every

rumour an interesting piece of information that may or may not be true
distorted twisted
tractable controllable
savage wild
to devour [dɪˈvaʊər] to eat
pail *Eimer*
hunter horse used in hunting
to refuse *here*: *verweigern*
astonishing surprising
to contain sb.'s rage to control sb.'s anger
contemptible [kənˈtemptəbəl] *verachtungswürdig*
flogging beating
irrepressible unable to stop
to whistle *pfeifen*
to coo *gurren*
elm *Ulme*
din sound
smithy *Schmiede*
doom death and destruction; *Untergang*
whirling *im Schwarm*
to alight to land
to launch to start
dung *Kot*
to peck to hack with a beak
vicious aggressive
calf (pl. calves) lower back part of the leg
skirmishing small fight
to prod to poke

side, while Benjamin turned around and lashed at them with his small hoofs. But once again the men, with their sticks and their hobnailed boots, were too strong for them; and suddenly, at a squeal from Snowball, which was the signal for retreat, all the animals turned and fled through the gateway into the yard.

The men gave a shout of triumph. They saw, as they imagined, their enemies in flight, and they rushed after them in disorder. This was just what Snowball had intended. As soon as they were well inside the yard, the three horses, the three cows and the rest of the pigs, who had been lying in ambush in the cowshed, suddenly emerged in their rear, cutting them off. Snowball now gave the signal for the charge. He himself dashed straight for Jones. Jones saw him coming, raised his gun and fired. The pellets scored bloody streaks along Snowball's back, and a sheep dropped dead. Without halting for an instant, Snowball flung his fifteen stone against Jones's legs. Jones was hurled into a pile of dung and his gun flew out of his hands. But the most terrifying spectacle of all was Boxer, rearing up on his hind legs and striking out with his great iron-shod hoofs like a stallion. His very first blow took a stable-lad from Foxwood on the skull and stretched him lifeless in the mud. At the sight, several men dropped their sticks and tried to run. Panic overtook them, and the next moment all the animals together were chasing them round and round the yard. They were gored, kicked, bitten, trampled on. There was not an animal on the farm that did not take vengeance on them after his own fashion. Even the cat suddenly leapt off a roof on to a cowman's shoulders and sank her claws in his neck, at which he yelled horribly. At a moment when the opening was clear, the men were glad enough to rush out of the yard and make a bolt for the main road. And so within five minutes of their invasion they were in ignominious retreat by the same way as they had come, with a flock of geese hissing after them and pecking at their calves all the way.

All the men were gone except one. Back in the yard Boxer was pawing with his hoof at the stable-lad, who lay face down in the mud, trying to turn him over. The boy did not stir.

"He is dead," said Boxer sorrowfully. "I had no intention of doing that. I forgot that I was wearing iron shoes. Who will believe that I did not do this on purpose?"

"No sentimentality, comrade!" cried Snowball, from whose wounds the blood was still dripping. "War is war. The only good human being is a dead one."

"I have no wish to take life, not even human life," repeated Boxer, and his eyes were full of tears.

"Where is Mollie?" exclaimed somebody.

to lash at to kick
hobnailed *genagelt*
retreat *Rückzug*
to lie in ambush to hide before a surprise attack
to emerge to appear suddenly
in sb.'s rear from behind
to cut off to block, to obstruct
charge sudden attack
to dash for to rush towards
to score to cut
stone unit of weight, 6.35 kg
to hurl to throw violently
to rear up to stand up
stallion male horse
blow firm knock
skull the bone that forms the head
to stretch to lay out
to gore to pierce with sth. sharp, like a horn
vengeance [ˈvendʒəns] revenge
after sb.'s own fashion in sb.'s own way
to yell to scream
to make a bolt to run off fast
ignominious [ˌɪɡnəˈmɪniəs] (*fml.*) shameful
flock *Schar*
to paw to touch with one's foot
to do sth. on purpose to do sth. intentionally
to cry to speak loudly
to exclaim to speak loudly

Mollie in fact was missing. For a moment there was great alarm; it was feared that the men might have harmed her in some way, or even carried her off with them. In the end, however, she was found hiding in her stall with her head buried among the hay in the manger. She had taken to flight as soon as the gun went off. And when the others came back from looking for her, it was to find that the stable-lad, who in fact was only stunned, had already recovered and made off.

manger ['meɪn(d)ʒə] box for animal food
to take to flight to run away
to stun to make unconscious
to make off to escape

The animals had now reassembled in the wildest excitement, each recounting his own exploits in the battle at the top of his voice. An impromptu celebration of the victory was held immediately. The flag was run up and 'Beasts of England' was sung a number of times, then the sheep who had been killed was given a solemn funeral, a hawthorn bush being planted on her grave. At the graveside Snowball made a little speech, emphasizing the need for all animals to be ready to die for Animal Farm if need be. The animals decided unanimously to create a military decoration, 'Animal Hero, First Class', which was conferred there and then on Snowball and Boxer. It consisted of a brass medal (they were really some old horse-brasses which had been found in the harness-room), to be worn on Sundays and holidays. There was also 'Animal Hero, Second Class', which was conferred posthumously on the dead sheep.

to recount to retell
exploit heroic deed
impromptu spontaneous
solemn *feierlich*
hawthorn *Weißdorn*
to confer to give a medal or award
brass *Messing*
horse brass *Zaumzeugbeschlag*
harness *Geschirr*
posthumous ['pɒstʃəməs] after sb.'s death

There was much discussion as to what the battle should be called. In the end, it was named the Battle of the Cowshed, since that was where the ambush had been sprung. Mr Jones's gun had been found lying in the mud, and it was known that there was a supply of cartridges in the farmhouse. It was decided to set the gun up at the foot of the flagstaff, like a piece of artillery, and to fire it twice a year – once on October the twelfth, the anniversary of the Battle of the Cowshed, and once on Midsummer Day, the anniversary of the Rebellion.

to spring (sprung, sprung) to start quickly
cartridge bullet
anniversary *Jahrestag*

Chapter V

As winter drew on, Mollie became more and more troublesome. She was late for work every morning and excused herself by saying that she had overslept, and she complained of mysterious pains, although her appetite was excellent. On every kind of pretext she would run away from work and go to the drinking pool, where she would stand foolishly gazing at her own reflection in the water. But there were also rumours of something more serious. One day as Mollie strolled blithely into the yard, flirting her long tail and chewing at a stalk of hay, Clover took her aside. "Mollie," she said, "I have something very serious to say to you. This morning I saw you looking over the hedge that divides Animal Farm from Foxwood. One of Mr Pilkington's men was standing on the other side of the hedge. And – I was a long way away, but I am almost certain I saw this – he was talking to you and you were allowing him to stroke your nose. What does that mean, Mollie?"

"He didn't! I wasn't! It isn't true!" cried Mollie, beginning to prance about and paw the ground.

"Mollie! Look me in the face. Do you give me your word of honour that that man was not stroking your nose?"

"It isn't true!" repeated Mollie, but she could not look Clover in the face, and the next moment she took to her heels and galloped away into the field.

A thought struck Clover. Without saying anything to the others, she went to Mollie's stall and turned over the straw with her hoof. Hidden under the straw was a little pile of lump sugar and several bunches of ribbon of different colours.

Three days later Mollie disappeared. For some weeks nothing was known of her whereabouts, then the pigeons reported that they had seen her on the other side of Willingdon. She was between the shafts of a smart dogcart painted red and black, which was standing outside a public-house. A fat red-faced man in check breeches and gaiters, who looked like a publican, was stroking her nose and feeding her with sugar. Her coat was newly clipped and she wore a scarlet ribbon round her forelock. She appeared to be enjoying herself, so the pigeons said. None of the animals ever mentioned Mollie again.

In January there came bitterly hard weather. The earth was like iron, and nothing could be done in the fields. Many meetings were held in the big barn, and the pigs occupied themselves with planning out the work of the coming season. It had come to be accepted that the pigs, who were manifestly cleverer than the

to draw on (drew, drawn) to approach
troublesome causing trouble
pretext excuse
foolish lacking intelligence
to gaze to look (dreamily)
to stroll to walk slowly; *gemächlich gehen*
blithe [blaɪð] happy
to stroke to move one's hand gently over
to prance *tänzeln*
whereabouts the place where sb. or sth. is
shaft *Deichsel*
dogcart *zweirädriger Einspanner*
public-house pub
check breeches *karierte Reithose*
gaiters *Gamaschen*
publican innkeeper
coat fur
to clip to cut
manifest clear

other animals, should decide all questions of farm policy, though their decisions had to be ratified by a majority vote. This arrangement would have worked well enough if it had not been for the disputes between Snowball and Napoleon. These two disagreed at every point where disagreement was possible. If one of them suggested sowing a bigger acreage with barley, the other was certain to demand a bigger acreage of oats, and if one of them said that such and such a field was just right for cabbages, the other would declare that it was useless for anything except roots. Each had his own following, and there were some violent debates. At the Meetings Snowball often won over the majority by his brilliant speeches, but Napoleon was better at canvassing support for himself in between times. He was especially successful with the sheep. Of late the sheep had taken to bleating 'Four legs good, two legs bad' both in and out of season, and they often interrupted the Meeting with this. It was noticed that they were especially liable to break into 'Four legs good, two legs bad' at crucial moments in Snowball's speeches. Snowball had made a close study of some back numbers of the *Farmer and Stockbreeder* which he had found in the farmhouse, and was full of plans for innovations and improvements. He talked learnedly about field drains, silage and basic slag, and had worked out a complicated scheme for all animals to drop their dung directly in the fields, at a different spot every day, to save the labour of cartage. Napoleon produced no schemes of his own, but said quietly that Snowball's would come to nothing, and seemed to be biding his time. But of all their controversies, none was so bitter as the one that took place over the windmill.

In the long pasture, not far from the farm buildings, there was a small knoll which was the highest point on the farm. After surveying the ground, Snowball declared that this was just the place for a windmill, which could be made to operate a dynamo and supply the farm with electrical power. This would light the stalls and warm them in winter, and would also run a circular saw, a chaff-cutter, a mangel-slicer, and an electric milking machine. The animals had never heard of anything of this kind before (for the farm was an old-fashioned one and had only the most primitive machinery), and they listened in astonishment while Snowball conjured up pictures of fantastic machines which would do their work for them while they grazed at their ease in the fields or improved their minds with reading and conversation.

Within a few weeks Snowball's plans for the windmill were fully worked out. The mechanical details came mostly from three books which had belonged to Mr Jones – *One Thousand Useful Things to Do About the House, Every Man His Own Bricklayer,*

to ratify to vote for sth., thereby making it legal
dispute argument
acreage area of land
cabbage *Kohl*
roots *Wurzelgemüse*
to canvass to ask for
liable likely
crucial ['kruːʃəl] important
back number old issue of a magazine
stockbreeder *Viehzüchter*
learned knowledgeable
drain *Entwässerungskanal*
silage ['saɪlɪdʒ] green food for animals that is kept in a silo
basic slag *Schlacke als Düngemittel*
cartage transport
to bide one's time to wait for the right moment
to survey to examine
circular saw *Kreissäge*
chaff-cutter *Häckselbank*
mangel-slicer red beet cutter
astonishment great surprise; *Erstaunen*
to conjure up to imagine
bricklayer *Maurer*

and *Electricity for Beginners*. Snowball used as his study a shed which had once been used for incubators and had a smooth wooden floor, suitable for drawing on. He was closeted there for hours at a time. With his books held open by a stone, and with a piece of chalk gripped between the knuckles of his trotter, he would move rapidly to and fro, drawing in line after line and uttering little whimpers of excitement. Gradually the plans grew into a complicated mass of cranks and cog-wheels, covering more than half the floor, which the other animals found completely unintelligible but very impressive. All of them came to look at Snowball's drawings at least once a day. Even the hens and ducks came, and were at pains not to tread on the chalk marks. Only Napoleon held aloof. He had declared himself against the windmill from the start. One day, however, he arrived unexpectedly to examine the plans. He walked heavily round the shed, looked closely at every detail of the plans and snuffed at them once or twice, then stood for a little while contemplating them out of the corner of his eye; then suddenly he lifted his leg, urinated over the plans and walked out without uttering a word. The whole farm was deeply divided on the subject of the windmill. Snowball did not deny that to build it would be a difficult business. Stone would have to be quarried and built up into walls, then the sails would have to be made and after that there would be need for dynamos and cables. (How these were to be procured, Snowball did not say.) But he maintained that it could all be done in a year. And thereafter, he declared, so much labour would be saved that the animals would only need to work three days a week. Napoleon, on the other hand, argued that the great need of the moment was to increase food production, and that if they wasted time on the windmill they would all starve to death. The animals formed themselves into two factions under the slogan, 'Vote for Snowball and the three-day week' and 'Vote for Napoleon and the full manger'. Benjamin was the only animal who did not side with either faction. He refused to believe either that food would become more plentiful or that the windmill would save work. Windmill or no windmill, he said, life would go on as it had always gone on – that is, badly.

Apart from the disputes over the windmill, there was the question of the defence of the farm. It was fully realized that though the human beings had been defeated in the Battle of the Cowshed they might make another and more determined attempt to recapture the farm and reinstate Mr Jones. They had all the more reason for doing so because the news of their defeat had spread across the countryside and made the animals on the neighbouring farms more restive than ever. As usual Snowball and Napo-

study home office
incubator *Brutkasten*
to be closeted *here*: to be shut in
crank *Kurbel, Hebel*
cog-wheel *Zahnrad*
unintelligible impossible to understand
to be at pains to try very hard
to hold aloof to stay away
to snuff at to breathe noisily to show dislike
to quarry to dig stone from a quarry *(Steinbruch)*
to procure to obtain
to starve to death to die of hunger
factions opposing groups
to side with to support
to recapture to get back by force
to reinstate [riːɪnˈsteɪt] to put sb. back into their former position
restive nervous

leon were in disagreement. According to Napoleon, what the animals must do was to procure firearms and train themselves in the use of them. According to Snowball, they must send out more and more pigeons and stir up rebellion among the animals on the other farms. The one argued that if they could not defend themselves they were bound to be conquered, the other argued that if rebellions happened everywhere they would have no need to defend themselves. The animals listened first to Napoleon, then to Snowball, and could not make up their minds which was right; indeed, they always found themselves in agreement with the one who was speaking at the moment.

At last the day came when Snowball's plans were completed. At the Meeting on the following Sunday the question of whether or not to begin work on the windmill was to be put to the vote. When the animals had assembled in the big barn, Snowball stood up and, though occasionally interrupted by bleating from the sheep, set forth his reasons for advocating the building of the windmill. Then Napoleon stood up to reply. He said very quietly that the windmill was nonsense and that he advised nobody to vote for it, and promptly sat down again; he had spoken for barely thirty seconds, and seemed almost indifferent as to the effect he produced. At this Snowball sprang to his feet, and shouting down the sheep, who had begun bleating again, broke into a passionate appeal in favour of the windmill. Until now the animals had been about equally divided in their sympathies, but in a moment Snowball's eloquence had carried them away. In glowing sentences he painted a picture of Animal Farm as it might be when sordid labour was lifted from the animals' backs. His imagination had now run far beyond chaff-cutters and turnip-slicers. Electricity, he said, could operate threshing machines, ploughs, harrows, rollers and reapers and binders, besides supplying every stall with its own electric light, hot and cold water, and an electric heater. By the time he had finished speaking, there was no doubt as to which way the vote would go. But just at this moment Napoleon stood up and, casting a peculiar sidelong look at Snowball, uttered a high-pitched whimper of a kind no one had ever heard him utter before.

At this there was a terrible baying sound outside, and nine enormous dogs wearing brass-studded collars came bounding into the barn. They dashed straight for Snowball, who only sprang from his place just in time to escape their snapping jaws. In a moment he was out of the door and they were after him. Too amazed and frightened to speak, all the animals crowded through the door to watch the chase. Snowball was racing across the long pasture that led to the road. He was running as only a pig can

to be bound to be certain

to advocate to recommend

indifferent not caring

passionate *leidenschaftlich*

eloquence ['eləkwəns] ability to speak well

sordid unpleasant

turnip-slicer *Rübenschneider*

harrow *Egge*
roller *Walze*
reaper *Mähmaschine*
binder *Mähbinder*

sidelong look out of the corner of your eye

baying sound the sound of barking dogs
brass-studded *mit Messing verziert*

jaw *Kiefer*

run, but the dogs were close on his heels. Suddenly he slipped and it seemed certain that they had him. Then he was up again, running faster than ever, then the dogs were gaining on him again. One of them all but closed his jaws on Snowball's tail, but Snowball whisked it free just in time. Then he put on an extra spurt and, with a few inches to spare, slipped through a hole in the hedge and was seen no more.

Silent and terrified, the animals crept back into the barn. In a moment the dogs came bounding back. At first no one had been able to imagine where these creatures came from, but the problem was soon solved: they were the puppies whom Napoleon had taken away from their mothers and reared privately. Though not yet full-grown, they were huge dogs, and as fierce-looking as wolves. They kept close to Napoleon. It was noticed that they wagged their tails to him in the same way as the other dogs had been used to do to Mr Jones.

Napoleon, with the dogs following him, now mounted on to the raised portion of the floor where Major had previously stood to deliver his speech. He announced that from now on the Sunday-morning Meetings would come to an end. They were unnecessary, he said, and wasted time. In future all questions relating to the working of the farm would be settled by a special committee of pigs, presided over by himself. These would meet in private and afterwards communicate their decisions to the others. The animals would still assemble on Sunday mornings to salute the flag, sing "Beasts of England", and receive their orders for the week; but there would be no more debates.

In spite of the shock that Snowball's expulsion had given them, the animals were dismayed by this announcement. Several of them would have protested if they could have found the right arguments. Even Boxer was vaguely troubled. He set his ears back, shook his forelock several times, and tried hard to marshal his thoughts; but in the end he could not think of anything to say. Some of the pigs themselves, however, were more articulate. Four young porkers in the front row uttered shrill squeals of disapproval, and all four of them sprang to their feet and began speaking at once. But suddenly the dogs sitting round Napoleon let out deep, menacing growls, and the pigs fell silent and sat down again. Then the sheep broke out into a tremendous bleating of 'Four legs good, two legs bad!' which went on for nearly a quarter of an hour and put an end to any chance of discussion.

Afterwards Squealer was sent round the farm to explain the new arrangement to the others.

"Comrades," he said, "I trust that every animal here appreciates the sacrifice that Comrade Napoleon has made in taking this extra

to gain on sb. to catch up with sb.
all but very nearly
to whisk to move quickly
spurt *Sprint*
to bound back to rush back
to rear to raise
to wag to move from side to side
to preside over (*fml.*) to be in charge of
expulsion the act of making sb. leave; *Vertreibung*
to be dismayed to be shocked
to marshal (*fml.*) to organize
menacing threatening
to appreciate to value
sacrifice sth. you give for sth. better

labour upon himself. Do not imagine, comrades, that leadership is a pleasure! On the contrary, it is a deep and heavy responsibility. No one believes more firmly than Comrade Napoleon that all animals are equal. He would be only too happy to let you make your decisions for yourselves. But sometimes you might make the wrong decisions, comrades, and then where should we be? Suppose you had decided to follow Snowball, with his moonshine of windmills – Snowball, who, as we now know, was no better than a criminal?"

moonshine (*infml.*) *here*: nonsense

"He fought bravely at the Battle of the Cowshed," said somebody.

"Bravery is not enough," said Squealer. "Loyalty and obedience are more important. And as to the Battle of the Cowshed, I believe the time will come when we shall find that Snowball's part in it was much exaggerated. Discipline, comrades, iron discipline! That is the watchword for today. One false step, and our enemies would be upon us. Surely, comrades, you do not want Jones back?"

obedience [ə'bi:diəns] doing what sb. is told

watchword slogan

Once again this argument was unanswerable. Certainly the animals did not want Jones back; if the holding of debates on Sunday mornings was liable to bring him back, then the debates must stop. Boxer, who had now had time to think things over, voiced the general feeling by saying: "If Comrade Napoleon says it, it must be right." And from then on he adopted the maxim, "Napoleon is always right," in addition to his private motto of "I will work harder."

to be liable to to be likely to

By this time the weather had broken and the spring ploughing had begun. The shed where Snowball had drawn his plans of the windmill had been shut up and it was assumed that the plans had been rubbed off the floor. Every Sunday morning at ten o'clock the animals assembled in the big barn to receive their orders for the week. The skull of old Major, now clean of flesh, had been disinterred from the orchard and set up on a stump at the foot of the flagstaff, beside the gun. After the hoisting of the flag, the animals were required to file past the skull in a reverent manner before entering the barn. Nowadays they did not sit all together as they had done in the past. Napoleon, with Squealer and another pig named Minimus, who had a remarkable gift for composing songs and poems, sat on the front of the raised platform, with the nine young dogs forming a semicircle round them, and the other pigs sitting behind. The rest of the animals sat facing them in the main body of the barn. Napoleon read out the orders for the week in a gruff soldierly style, and after a single singing of 'Beasts of England', all the animals dispersed.

to assume *annehmen*

to disinter [dɪs.ɪn'tɜːr] (*fml.*) to dig up

stump *Stumpf*

to file past to walk by

reverent respectful

semicircle half-circle

gruff rough

to disperse to leave in different directions

On the third Sunday after Snowball's expulsion, the animals were somewhat surprised to hear Napoleon announce that the windmill was to be built after all. He did not give any reason for having changed his mind, but merely warned the animals that this extra task would mean very hard work, it might even be necessary to reduce their rations. The plans, however, had all been prepared, down to the last detail. A special committee of pigs had been at work upon them for the past three weeks. The building of the windmill with various other improvements, was expected to take two years.

That evening Squealer explained privately to the other animals that Napoleon had never in reality been opposed to the windmill. On the contrary, it was he who had advocated it in the beginning, and the plan which Snowball had drawn on the floor of the incubator shed had actually been stolen from among Napoleon's papers. The windmill was, in fact, Napoleon's own creation. Why, then, asked somebody, had he spoken so strongly against it? Here Squealer looked very sly. That, he said, was Comrade Napoleon's cunning. He had *seemed* to oppose the windmill, simply as a manoeuvre to get rid of Snowball, who was a dangerous character and a bad influence. Now that Snowball was out of the way, the plan could go forward without his interference. This, said Squealer, was something called tactics. He repeated a number of times, "Tactics, comrades, tactics!" skipping round and whisking his tail with a merry laugh. The animals were not certain what the word meant, but Squealer spoke so persuasively, and the three dogs who happened to be with him growled so threateningly, that they accepted his explanation without further questions.

sly secretive; *listig*

cunning being able to get what you want by tricking or cheating

interference *Einmischung*

Chapter VI

to grudge *here*: to do sth. unwillingly

voluntary acting by choice

to absent oneself (*fml.*) to stay away; *fernbleiben*

limestone *Kalkstein*

outhouse building near the main building

pick *Spitzhacke*

crowbar *Brecheisen*

vain useless

gravity *Schwerkraft*

boulder large stone

bed bottom

to lash to tie tightly

desperate giving little hope of success

to topple over to push over

to shatter to break into many pieces

to yoke oneself into a cart *sich selbst Geschirr anlegen*

governess-cart *zweirädriges Pferdefuhrwerk*

superintendence supervision

laborious work intensive

exhausting costing a lot of energy

All that year the animals worked like slaves. But they were happy in their work; they grudged no effort or sacrifice, well aware that everything that they did was for the benefit of themselves and those of their kind who would come after them, and not for a pack of idle, thieving human beings.

Throughout the spring and summer they worked a sixty-hour week, and in August Napoleon announced that there would be work on Sunday afternoons as well. This work was strictly voluntary, but any animal who absented himself from it would have his rations reduced by half. Even so, it was found necessary to leave certain tasks undone. The harvest was a little less successful than in the previous year, and two fields which should have been sown with roots in the early summer were not sown because the ploughing had not been completed early enough. It was possible to foresee that the coming winter would be a hard one.

The windmill presented unexpected difficulties. There was a good quarry of limestone on the farm, and plenty of sand and cement had been found in one of the outhouses, so that all the materials for building were at hand. But the problem the animals could not at first solve was how to break up the stone into pieces of suitable size. There seemed no way of doing this except with picks and crowbars, which no animal could use, because no animal could stand on his hind legs. Only after weeks of vain effort did the right idea occur to somebody – namely, to utilize the force of gravity. Huge boulders, far too big to be used as they were, were lying all over the bed of the quarry. The animals lashed ropes round these, and then all together, cows, horses, sheep, any animal that could lay hold of the rope – even the pigs sometimes joined in at critical moments – they dragged them with desperate slowness up the slope to the top of the quarry, where they were toppled over the edge, to shatter to pieces below. Transporting the stone when it was once broken was comparatively simple. The horses carried it off in cartloads, the sheep dragged single blocks, even Muriel and Benjamin yoked themselves into an old governess-cart and did their share. By late summer a sufficient store of stone had accumulated, and then the building began, under the superintendence of the pigs.

But it was a slow, laborious process. Frequently it took a whole day of exhausting effort to drag a single boulder to the top of the quarry, and sometimes when it was pushed over the edge it failed to break. Nothing could have been achieved without Boxer, whose strength seemed equal to that of all the rest of the animals put together. When the boulder began to slip and the animals cried out in despair at finding themselves dragged down the hill, it was always Boxer who strained himself against the rope and brought the boulder to a stop. To see him toiling up the slope inch by inch, his breath coming fast, the tips of his hoofs clawing at the ground, and his great sides matted with sweat, filled everyone with admiration. Clover warned him sometimes to be careful not to overstrain himself, but Boxer would never listen to her. His two slogans, 'I will work harder' and 'Napoleon is always right', seemed to him a sufficient answer to all problems. He had made arrangements with the cockerel to call him three-quarters of an hour earlier in the mornings instead of half an hour. And in his spare moments, of which there were not many nowadays, he would go alone to the quarry, collect a load of broken stone, and drag it down to the site of the windmill unassisted.

The animals were not badly off throughout that summer, in spite of the hardness of their work. If they had no more food than they had had in Jones's day, at least they did not have less. The advantage of only having to feed themselves, and not having to support five extravagant human beings as well, was so great that it would have taken a lot of failures to outweigh it. And in many ways the animal method of doing things was more efficient and saved labour. Such jobs as weeding, for instance, could be done with a thoroughness impossible to human beings. And again, since no animal now stole, it was unnecessary to fence off pasture from arable land, which saved a lot of labour on the upkeep of hedges and gates. Nevertheless, as the summer wore on, various unforeseen shortages began to make themselves felt. There was need of paraffin oil, nails, string, dog biscuits and iron for the horses' shoes, none of which could be produced on the farm. Later there would also be need for seeds and artificial manures, besides various tools and, finally, the machinery for the windmill. How these were to be procured, no one was able to imagine.

One Sunday morning, when the animals assembled to receive their orders, Napoleon announced that he had decided upon a new policy. From now onwards Animal Farm would engage in trade with the neighbouring farms: not, of course, for any commercial purpose, but simply in order to obtain certain materials which were urgently necessary. The needs of the windmill must override everything else, he said. He was therefore making arrangements to sell a stack of hay and part of the current year's wheat crop, and later on, if more money were needed, it would have to be made up by the sale of eggs, for which there was always a market in Willingdon. The hens, said Napoleon, should

despair hopelessness

matted forming a thick mass; *verfilzt*
to overstrain to do more than you can handle

to outweigh to be more important or better

to weed *Unkraut jäten*

thoroughness ['θʌrənəs] completeness

arable suitable for growing crops

upkeep looking after

to wear on to pass slowly

paraffin oil *Petroleum*

manure animal waste that is used in fields to help plants grow

to override (overrode, overridden) *here*: to be more important than
stack *Stapel*

welcome this sacrifice as their own special contribution towards the building of the windmill.

Once again the animals were conscious of a vague uneasiness. Never to have any dealings with human beings, never to engage in trade, never to make use of money – had not these been among the earliest resolutions passed at that first triumphant Meeting after Jones was expelled? All the animals remembered passing such resolutions: or at least they thought that they remembered it. The four young pigs who had protested when Napoleon abolished the Meetings raised their voices timidly, but they were promptly silenced by a tremendous growling from the dogs. Then, as usual, the sheep broke into 'Four legs good, two legs bad!' and the momentary awkwardness was smoothed over. Finally Napoleon raised his trotter for silence and announced that he had already made all the arrangements. There would be no need for any of the animals to come in contact with human beings, which would clearly be most undesirable. He intended to take the whole burden upon his own shoulders. A Mr Whymper, a solicitor living in Willingdon, had agreed to act as intermediary between Animal Farm and the outside world, and would visit the farm every Monday morning to receive his instructions. Napoleon ended his speech with his usual cry of 'Long live Animal Farm!' and after the singing of 'Beasts of England' the animals were dismissed.

Afterwards Squealer made a round of the farm and set the animals' minds at rest. He assured them that the resolution against engaging in trade and using money had never been passed, or even suggested. It was pure imagination, probably traceable in the beginning to lies circulated by Snowball. A few animals still felt faintly doubtful, but Squealer asked them shrewdly, "Are you certain that this is not something that you have dreamed, comrades? Have you any record of such a resolution? Is it written down anywhere?" And since it was certainly true that nothing of the kind existed in writing, the animals were satisfied that they had been mistaken.

Every Monday Mr Whymper visited the farm as had been arranged. He was a sly-looking little man with side whiskers, a solicitor in a very small way of business, but sharp enough to have realized earlier than anyone else that Animal Farm would need a broker and that the commissions would be worth having. The animals watched his coming and going with a kind of dread, and avoided him as much as possible. Nevertheless, the sight of Napoleon, on all fours, delivering orders to Whymper, who stood on two legs, roused their pride and partly reconciled them to the new arrangement. Their relations with the human race were now

conscious [ˈkɒnʃəs] aware

timid shy, fearful

momentary lasting for a moment
awkwardness [ˈɔːkwədnəs] feeling of unpleasantness

solicitor lawyer
intermediary middle man

to dismiss sb. to allow sb. to leave

traceable to sth. *zurückführbar auf etw.*

shrewd clever; *schlau*

side whiskers *Koteletten*

broker agent who does business for other people
dread [dred] fear

to reconcile sb. to sth. [ˈrekənsaɪl] to make sb. accept a certain situation not quite the same as they had been before. The human beings did not hate Animal Farm any less now that it was prospering; indeed, they hated it more than ever. Every human being held it as an article of faith that the farm would go bankrupt sooner or later, and, above all, that the windmill would be a failure. They would meet in the public-houses and prove to one another by means of diagrams that the windmill was bound to fall down, or that if it did stand up, then that it would never work. And yet, against their will, they had developed a certain respect for the efficiency with which the animals were managing their own affairs. One symptom of this was that they had begun to call Animal Farm by its proper name and ceased to pretend that it was called the Manor Farm. They had also dropped their championship of Jones, who had given up hope of getting his farm back and gone to live in another part of the county. Except through Whymper, there was as yet no contact between Animal Farm and the outside world, but there were constant rumours that Napoleon was about to enter into a definite business agreement either with Mr Pilkington of Foxwood or with Mr Frederick of Pinchfield – but never, it was noticed, with both simultaneously.

It was about this time that the pigs suddenly moved into the farmhouse and took up their residence there. Again the animals seemed to remember that a resolution against this had been passed in the early days, and again Squealer was able to convince them that this was not the case. It was absolutely necessary, he said, that the pigs, who were the brains of the farm, should have a quiet place to work in. It was also more suited to the dignity of the Leader (for of late he had taken to speaking of Napoleon under the title of 'Leader') to live in a house than in a mere sty. Nevertheless, some of the animals were disturbed when they heard that the pigs not only took their meals in the kitchen and used the drawing-room as a recreation room, but also slept in the beds. Boxer passed it off as usual with "Napoleon is always right!", but Clover, who thought she remembered a definite ruling against beds, went to the end of the barn and tried to puzzle out the Seven Commandments which were inscribed there. Finding herself unable to read more than individual letters, she fetched Muriel.

"Muriel," she said, "read me the Fourth Commandment. Does it not say something about never sleeping in a bed?"

With some difficulty Muriel spelt it out.

"It says, 'No animal shall sleep in a bed *with sheets*'," she announced finally.

Curiously enough, Clover had not remembered that the Fourth Commandment mentioned sheets; but as it was there on the

to prosper to be successful

article of faith sth. you believe very strongly

to cease to stop

to drop one's championship of sb. to stop supporting sb.

simultaneous at the same time

sty stall where pigs are kept

wall, it must have done so. And Squealer, who happened to be passing at this moment, attended by two or three dogs, was able to put the whole matter in its proper perspective.

"You have heard, then, comrades," he said, "that we pigs now sleep in the beds of the farmhouse? And why not? You did not suppose, surely, that there was ever a ruling against *beds*? A bed merely means a place to sleep in. A pile of straw in a stall is a bed, properly regarded. The rule was against *sheets*, which are a human invention. We have removed the sheets from the farmhouse beds, and sleep between blankets. And very comfortable beds they are too! But not more comfortable than we need, I can tell you, comrades, with all the brainwork we have to do nowadays. You would not rob us of our repose, would you, comrades? You would not have us too tired to carry out our duties? Surely none of you wishes to see Jones back?"

repose (*fml.*) rest

The animals reassured him on this point immediately, and no more was said about the pigs sleeping in the farmhouse beds. And when, some days afterwards, it was announced that from now on the pigs would get up an hour later in the mornings than the other animals, no complaint was made about that either.

complaint a statement that sth. is not right or acceptable

By the autumn the animals were tired but happy. They had had a hard year, and after the sale of part of the hay and corn, the stores of food for the winter were none too plentiful, but the windmill compensated for everything. It was almost half built now. After the harvest there was a stretch of clear dry weather, and the animals toiled harder than ever, thinking it well worth while to plod to and fro all day with blocks of stone if by doing so they could raise the walls another foot. Boxer would even come out at nights and work for an hour or two on his own by the light of the harvest moon. In their spare moments the animals would walk round and round the half-finished mill, admiring the strength and perpendicularity of its walls and marvelling that they should ever have been able to build anything so imposing. Only old Benjamin refused to grow enthusiastic about the windmill, though, as usual, he would utter nothing beyond the cryptic remark that donkeys live a long time.

to plod to walk in a slow and tired way

spare moment time off

perpendicularity [ˌpɜːpənˈdɪkjələriti] straightness
to marvel to be impressed
imposing impressive

November came, with raging south-west winds. Building had to stop because it was now too wet to mix the cement. Finally there came a night when the gale was so violent that the farm buildings rocked on their foundations and several tiles were blown off the roof of the barn. The hens woke up squawking with terror because they had all dreamed simultaneously of hearing a gun go off in the distance. In the morning the animals came out of their stalls to find that the flagstaff had been blown down and an elm tree at the foot of the orchard had been plucked up like a radish.

gale extremely strong wind

tile *Dachziegel*

to squawk [skwɔːk] to cry loudly and unpleasantly

to pluck up to pull out
radish *Rettich*

They had just noticed this when a cry of despair broke from every animal's throat. A terrible sight had met their eyes. The windmill was in ruins.

With one accord they dashed down to the spot. Napoleon, who seldom moved out of a walk, raced ahead of them all. Yes, there it lay, the fruit of all their struggles, levelled to its foundations, the stones they had broken and carried so laboriously scattered all around. Unable at first to speak, they stood gazing mournfully at the litter of fallen stone. Napoleon paced to and fro in silence, occasionally snuffing at the ground. His tail had grown rigid and twitched sharply from side to side, a sign in him of intense mental activity. Suddenly he halted as though his mind were made up. "Comrades," he said quietly, "do you know who is responsible for this? Do you know the enemy who has come in the night and overthrown our windmill? Snowball!" he suddenly roared in a voice of thunder. "Snowball has done this thing! In sheer malignity, thinking to set back our plans and avenge himself for his ignominious expulsion, this traitor has crept here under cover of night and destroyed our work of nearly a year. Comrades, here and now I pronounce the death sentence upon Snowball. 'Animal Hero, Second Class', and half a bushel of apples to any animal who brings him to justice. A full bushel to anyone who captures him alive!"

The animals were shocked beyond measure to learn that even Snowball could be guilty of such an action. There was a cry of indignation, and everyone began thinking out ways of catching Snowball if he should ever come back. Almost immediately the footprints of a pig were discovered in the grass at a little distance from the knoll. They could only be traced for a few yards, but appeared to lead to a hole in the hedge. Napoleon snuffed deeply at them and pronounced them to be Snowball's. He gave it as his opinion that Snowball had probably come from the direction of Foxwood Farm.

"No more delays, comrades!" cried Napoleon when the footprints had been examined. "There is work to be done. This very morning we begin rebuilding the windmill, and we will build all through the winter, rain or shine. We will teach this miserable traitor that he cannot undo our work so easily. Remember, comrades, there must be no alteration in our plans: they shall be carried out to the day. Forward, comrades! Long live the windmill! Long live Animal Farm!"

to level to flatten

mournful very sad

litter mess

to snuff to smell, to sniff

rigid stiff

to twitch to move suddenly

malignity [məˈlɪgnəti] evil

to avenge oneself to take revenge

ignominious (*fml.*) that makes you feel ashamed

expulsion the act of forcing sb. to leave a place

traitor sb. who betrays a person's trust

to creep (crept, crept) *schleichen*

indignation feeling of being treated unfairly

alteration change

Chapter VII

sleet mixture of snow and rain

envious [ˈenviəs] jealous

to rejoice to express great happiness

out of spite in order to hurt or upset sb.

snowdrift *Schneeverwehung*

to lose heart to give up on sth.

to fall (fell, fallen) **short** to be less than enough

clamp pile of earth that you store potatoes in

edible able to be eaten

mangel *Rübe*

vitally absolutely

to conceal to hide

to embolden to make sb. brave or confident

to put about to spread

famine hunger

to resort to sth. to turn to sth.

infanticide crime of killing a baby

hitherto (*fml.*) until now

It was a bitter winter. The stormy weather was followed by sleet and snow, and then by a hard frost which did not break till well into February. The animals carried on as best they could with the rebuilding of the windmill, well knowing that the outside world was watching them and that the envious human beings would rejoice and triumph if the mill were not finished on time.

Out of spite, the human beings pretended not to believe that it was Snowball who had destroyed the windmill: they said that it had fallen down because the walls were too thin. The animals knew that this was not the case. Still, it had been decided to build the walls three feet thick this time instead of eighteen inches as before, which meant collecting much larger quantities of stone. For a long time the quarry was full of snowdrifts and nothing could be done. Some progress was made in the dry frosty weather that followed, but it was cruel work, and the animals could not feel so hopeful about it as they had felt before. They were always cold, and usually hungry as well. Only Boxer and Clover never lost heart. Squealer made excellent speeches on the joy of service and the dignity of labour, but the other animals found more inspiration in Boxer's strength and his never-failing cry of "I will work harder!".

In January food fell short. The corn ration was drastically reduced, and it was announced that an extra potato ration would be issued to make up for it. Then it was discovered that the greater part of the potato crop had been frosted in the clamps, which had not been covered thickly enough. The potatoes had become soft and discoloured, and only a few were edible. For days at a time the animals had nothing to eat but chaff and mangels. Starvation seemed to stare them in the face.

It was vitally necessary to conceal this fact from the outside world. Emboldened by the collapse of the windmill, the human beings were inventing fresh lies about Animal Farm. Once again it was being put about that all the animals were dying of famine and disease, and that they were continually fighting among themselves and had resorted to cannibalism and infanticide. Napoleon was well aware of the bad results that might follow if the real facts of the food situation were known, and he decided to make use of Mr Whymper to spread a contrary impression. Hitherto the animals had had little or no contact with Whymper on his weekly visits: now, however, a few selected animals, mostly sheep, were instructed to remark casually in his hearing that rations had been increased. In addition, Napoleon ordered the almost empty bins in the store-shed to be filled nearly to the brim with sand, which was then covered up with what remained of the grain and meal. On some suitable pretext Whymper was led through the store-shed and allowed to catch a glimpse of the bins. He was deceived, and continued to report to the outside world that there was no food shortage on Animal Farm.

Nevertheless, towards the end of January it became obvious that it would be necessary to procure some more grain from somewhere. In these days Napoleon rarely appeared in public, but spent all his time in the farmhouse, which was guarded at each door by fierce-looking dogs. When he did emerge, it was in a ceremonial manner, with an escort of six dogs who closely surrounded him and growled if anyone came too near. Frequently he did not even appear on Sunday mornings, but issued his orders through one of the other pigs, usually Squealer.

One Sunday morning Squealer announced that the hens, who had just come in to lay again, must surrender their eggs. Napoleon had accepted, through Whymper, a contract for four hundred eggs a week. The price of these would pay for enough grain and meal to keep the farm going till summer came on and conditions were easier.

When the hens heard this, they raised a terrible outcry. They had been warned earlier that this sacrifice might be necessary, but had not believed that it would really happen. They were just getting their clutches ready for the spring sitting, and they protested that to take the eggs away now was murder. For the first time since the expulsion of Jones, there was something resembling a rebellion. Led by three young Black Minorca pullets, the hens made a determined effort to thwart Napoleon's wishes. Their method was to fly up to the rafters and there lay their eggs, which smashed to pieces on the floor. Napoleon acted swiftly and ruthlessly. He ordered the hens' rations to be stopped, and decreed that any animal giving so much as a grain of corn to a hen should be punished by death. The dogs saw to it that these orders were carried out. For five days the hens held out, then they capitulated and went back to their nesting boxes. Nine hens had died in the meantime. Their bodies were buried in the orchard, and it was given out that they had died of coccidiosis. Whymper heard nothing of this affair, and the eggs were duly delivered, a grocer's van driving up to the farm once a week to take them away.

All this while no more had been seen of Snowball. He was rumoured to be hiding on one of the neighbouring farms, either Foxwood or Pinchfield. Napoleon was by this time on slightly better terms with the other farmers than before. It happened that

brim top
meal *Mehl*
to procure (*fml.*) to get
to surrender to hand over
outcry loud expression of protest
clutch collection of eggs
sitting *Brutzeit*
to resemble sth. to be or look like sth. else
pullet young hen
to thwart (*fml.*) to prevent from achieving sth.
ruthless cruel
to decree [dɪˈkriː] to order
to give out to announce publicly
coccidiosis disease affecting hens

timber wood
beech spinney *Buchendickicht*
well seasoned dried
anxious [ˈæŋkʃəs] wanting sth. very much
to hesitate to pause because you are unsure about sth.

there was in the yard a pile of timber which had been stacked there ten years earlier when a beech spinney was cleared. It was well seasoned, and Whymper had advised Napoleon to sell it; both Mr Pilkington and Mr Frederick were anxious to buy it. Napoleon was hesitating between the two, unable to make up his mind. It was noticed that whenever he seemed on the point of coming to an agreement with Frederick, Snowball was declared to be in hiding at Foxwood, while, when he inclined towards Pilkington, Snowball was said to be at Pinchfield.

to frequent [frɪˈkwent] (*fml.*) to visit
mischief trouble
to gnaw to chew
bark *Rinde*
to attribute sth. to sb. to hold sb. responsible for sth.
mislaid *verlegt*
to be in league with sb. to make (secret) plans with sb.

Suddenly, early in the spring, an alarming thing was discovered. Snowball was secretly frequenting the farm by night! The animals were so disturbed that they could hardly sleep in their stalls. Every night, it was said, he came creeping in under cover of darkness and performed all kinds of mischief. He stole the corn, he upset the milk-pails, he broke the eggs, he trampled the seed-beds, he gnawed the bark off the fruit trees. Whenever anything went wrong it became usual to attribute it to Snowball. If a window was broken or a drain was blocked up, someone was certain to say that Snowball had come in the night and done it, and when the key of the store-shed was lost, the whole farm was convinced that Snowball had thrown it down the well. Curiously enough, they went on believing this even after the mislaid key was found under a sack of meal. The cows declared unanimously that Snowball crept into their stalls and milked them in their sleep. The rats, which had been troublesome that winter, were also said to be in league with Snowball.

trace *Spur*
snout nose of an animal
blood-curdling terrifying

Napoleon decreed that there should be a full investigation into Snowball's activities. With his dogs in attendance he set out and made a careful tour of inspection of the farm buildings, the other animals following at a respectful distance. At every few steps Napoleon stopped and snuffed the ground for traces of Snowball's footsteps, which, he said, he could detect by the smell. He snuffed in every corner, in the barn, in the cowshed, in the henhouses, in the vegetable garden, and found traces of Snowball almost everywhere. He would put his snout to the ground, give several deep sniffs, and exclaim in a terrible voice, "Snowball! He has been here! I can smell him distinctly!", and at the word 'Snowball' all the dogs let out blood-curdling growls and showed their side teeth.

to pervade to spread through every part of sth.
to menace (*fml.*) to threaten; *bedrohen*

The animals were thoroughly frightened. It seemed to them as though Snowball were some kind of invisible influence, pervading the air about them and menacing them with all kinds of dangers. In the evening Squealer called them together, and with an alarmed expression on his face told them that he had some serious news to report.

"Comrades!" cried Squealer, making little nervous skips, "a most terrible thing has been discovered. Snowball has sold himself to Frederick of Pinchfield Farm, who is even now plotting to attack us and take our farm away from us! Snowball is to act as his guide when the attack begins. But there is worse than that. We had thought that Snowball's rebellion was caused simply by his vanity and ambition. But we were wrong, comrades. Do you know what the real reason was? Snowball was in league with Jones from the very start! He was Jones's secret agent all the time. It has all been proved by documents which he left behind him and which we have only just discovered. To my mind this explains a great deal, comrades. Did we not see for ourselves how he attempted – fortunately without success – to get us defeated and destroyed at the Battle of the Cowshed?"

The animals were stupefied. This was a wickedness far outdoing Snowball's destruction of the windmill. But it was some minutes before they could fully take it in. They all remembered, or thought they remembered, how they had seen Snowball charging ahead of them at the Battle of the Cowshed, how he had rallied and encouraged them at every turn, and how he had not paused for an instant even when the pellets from Jones's gun had wounded his back. At first it was a little difficult to see how this fitted in with his being on Jones's side. Even Boxer, who seldom asked questions, was puzzled. He lay down, tucked his fore hoofs beneath him, shut his eyes, and with a hard effort managed to formulate his thoughts.

"I do not believe that," he said. "Snowball fought bravely at the Battle of the Cowshed. I saw him myself. Did we not give him 'Animal Hero, first Class', immediately afterwards?"

"That was our mistake, comrade. For we know now – it is all written down in the secret documents that we have found – that in reality he was trying to lure us to our doom."

"But he was wounded," said Boxer. "We all saw him running with blood."

"That was part of the arrangement!" cried Squealer. "Jones's shot only grazed him. I could show you this in his own writing, if you were able to read it. The plot was for Snowball, at the critical moment, to give the signal for flight and leave the field to the enemy. And he very nearly succeeded – I will even say, comrades, he *would* have succeeded if it had not been for our heroic Leader, Comrade Napoleon. Do you not remember how, just at the moment when Jones and his men had got inside the yard, Snowball suddenly turned and fled, and many animals followed him? And do you not remember, too, that it was just at that moment, when panic was spreading and all seemed lost, that Com-

to plot to plan secretly

vanity (too much) pride in your own accomplishment or ability

stupefied shocked and unable to think
wickedness evil
to take sth. in to understand sth.
to charge to attack
to rally to energize
at every turn everywhere and always
to encourage to motivate

puzzled confused

to formulate to express

to lure to trap; *locken*
doom ruin

to graze to touch lightly

rade Napoleon sprang forward with a cry of 'Death to Humanity!' and sank his teeth in Jones's leg? Surely you remember *that*, comrades?" exclaimed Squealer, frisking from side to side.

Now when Squealer described the scene so graphically, it seemed to the animals that they did remember it. At any rate, they remembered that at the critical moment of the battle Snowball had turned to flee. But Boxer was still a little uneasy.

"I do not believe that Snowball was a traitor at the beginning," he said finally. "What he has done since is different. But I believe that at the Battle of the Cowshed he was a good comrade."

"Our Leader, Comrade Napoleon," announced Squealer, speaking very slowly and firmly, "has stated categorically – categorically, comrade – that Snowball was Jones's agent from the very beginning – yes, and from long before the Rebellion was ever thought of."

"Ah, that is different!" said Boxer. "If Comrade Napoleon says it, it must be right."

"That is the true spirit, comrade!" cried Squealer, but it was noticed he cast a very ugly look at Boxer with his little twinkling eyes. He turned to go, then paused and added impressively: "I warn every animal on this farm to keep his eyes very wide open. For we have reason to think that some of Snowball's secret agents are lurking among us at this moment!"

Four days later, in the late afternoon, Napoleon ordered all the animals to assemble in the yard. When they were all gathered together, Napoleon emerged from the farmhouse, wearing both his medals (for he had recently awarded himself 'Animal Hero, First Class' and 'Animal Hero, Second Class'), with his nine huge dogs frisking round him and uttering growls that sent shivers down all the animals' spines. They all cowered silently in their places, seeming to know in advance that some terrible thing was about to happen.

Napoleon stood sternly surveying his audience; then he uttered a high-pitched whimper. Immediately the dogs bounded forward, seized four of the pigs by the ear and dragged them, squealing with pain and terror, to Napoleon's feet. The pigs' ears were bleeding, the dogs had tasted blood, and for a few moments they appeared to go quite mad. To the amazement of everybody, three of them flung themselves upon Boxer. Boxer saw them coming and put out his great hoof, caught a dog in mid-air, and pinned him to the ground. The dog shrieked for mercy and the other two fled with their tails between their legs. Boxer looked at Napoleon to know whether he should crush the dog to death or let it go. Napoleon appeared to change countenance, and sharply ordered Boxer to let the dog go, whereat Boxer lifted his hoof, and the dog slunk away, bruised and howling.

to frisk to jump about
graphic clear and detailed
ugly nasty, evil
to lurk to wait in hiding
to send shivers down one's spine *Schauer über den Rücken laufen lassen*
to cower to stay still out of fear; *sich ducken*
stern serious
amazement surprise
to shriek to cry out loud; *schreien*
mercy *Gnade*
to crush to press very hard
countenance (*fml.*) expression
whereat (*old use*) as a result of which
to slink (slunk, slunk) to walk away quietly
bruised injured

Presently the tumult died down. The four pigs waited, trembling, with guilt written on every line of their countenances. Napoleon now called upon them to confess their crimes. They were the same four pigs as had protested when Napoleon abolished the Sunday Meetings. Without any further prompting they confessed that they had been secretly in touch with Snowball ever since his expulsion, that they had collaborated with him in destroying the windmill, and that they had entered into an agreement with him to hand over Animal Farm to Mr Frederick. They added that Snowball had privately admitted to them that he had been Jones's secret agent for years past. When they had finished their confession, the dogs promptly tore their throats out, and in a terrible voice Napoleon demanded whether any other animal had anything to confess.

The three hens who had been the ringleaders in the attempted rebellion over the eggs now came forward and stated that Snowball had appeared to them in a dream and incited them to disobey Napoleon's orders. They, too, were slaughtered. Then a goose came forward and confessed to having secreted six ears of corn during the last year's harvest and eaten them in the night. Then a sheep confessed to having urinated in the drinking pool – urged to do this, so she said, by Snowball – and two other sheep confessed to having murdered an old ram, an especially devoted follower of Napoleon, by chasing him round and round a bonfire when he was suffering from a cough. They were all slain on the spot. And so the tale of confessions and executions went on, until there was a pile of corpses lying before Napoleon's feet and the air was heavy with the smell of blood, which had been unknown there since the expulsion of Jones.

When it was all over, the remaining animals, except for the pigs and dogs, crept away in a body. They were shaken and miserable. They did not know which was more shocking – the treachery of the animals who had leagued themselves with Snowball, or the cruel retribution they had just witnessed. In the old days there had often been scenes of bloodshed equally terrible, but it seemed to all of them that it was far worse now that it was happening among themselves. Since Jones had left the farm, until today, no animal had killed another animal. Not even a rat had been killed. They had made their way on to the little knoll where the half-finished windmill stood, and with one accord they all lay down as though huddling together for warmth – Clover, Muriel, Benjamin, the cows, the sheep and a whole flock of geese and hens – everyone, indeed, except the cat, who had suddenly disappeared just before Napoleon ordered the animals to assemble. For some time nobody spoke. Only Boxer remained on his feet. He fidgeted

to confess to admit that you have done wrong

prompting *Aufforderung*

to incite to encourage

to secrete (*fml.*) to take away secretly

ear top part of a grain plant; *Ähre*

ram *Widder*

bonfire *Lagerfeuer*

cough [kɒf] *Husten*

execution killing as punishment

corpse dead body

treachery the fact of going behind sb.'s back; *Verrat*

to league oneself with to join up with

retribution punishment

bloodshed violence and death

to huddle together *zusammenkauern*

to fidget to keep moving nervously

to swish sth. to move sth. quickly through the air

to lumber to move heavily and noisily

successive [sək'sesɪv] one after the other without a break

to curl to move in a twisted shape

bursting *aufblühend*

to gild to cover in shining, golden colour

fierce angry and aggressive

to roam to wander

to and fro, swishing his long black tail against his sides and occasionally uttering a little whinny of surprise. Finally he said: "I do not understand it. I would not have believed that such things could happen on our farm. It must be due to some fault in ourselves. The solution, as I see it, is to work harder. From now onwards I shall get up a full hour earlier in the mornings."

And he moved off at his lumbering trot and made for the quarry. Having got there, he collected two successive loads of stone and dragged them down to the windmill before retiring for the night.

The animals huddled about Clover, not speaking. The knoll where they were lying gave them a wide prospect across the countryside. Most of Animal Farm was within their view – the long pasture stretching down to the main road, the hayfield, the spinney, the drinking pool, the ploughed fields where the young wheat was thick and green, and the red roofs of the farm buildings with the smoke curling from the chimneys. It was a clear spring evening. The grass and the bursting hedges were gilded by the level rays of the sun. Never had the farm – and with a kind of surprise they remembered that it was their own farm, every inch of it their own property – appeared to the animals so desirable a place. As Clover looked down the hillside her eyes filled with tears. If she could have spoken her thoughts, it would have been to say that this was not what they had aimed at when they had set themselves years ago to work for the overthrow of the human race. These scenes of terror and slaughter were not what they had looked forward to on that night when old Major first stirred them to rebellion. If she herself had had any picture of the future, it had been of a society of animals set free from hunger and the whip, all equal, each working according to his capacity, the strong protecting the weak, as she had protected the lost brood of ducklings with her foreleg on the night of Major's speech. Instead – she did not know why – they had come to a time when no one dared speak his mind, when fierce, growling dogs roamed everywhere, and when you had to watch your comrades torn to pieces after confessing to shocking crimes. There was no thought of rebellion or disobedience in her mind. She knew that, even as things were, they were far better off than they had been in the days of Jones, and that before all else it was needful to prevent the return of the human beings. Whatever happened she would remain faithful, work hard, carry out the orders that were given to her and accept the leadership of Napoleon. But still, it was not for this that she and all the other animals had hoped and toiled. It was not for this that they had built the windmill and faced the bullets of Jones's gun. Such were her thoughts, though she lacked the words to express them.

At last, feeling this to be in some way a substitute for the words she was unable to find, she began to sing 'Beasts of England'. The other animals sitting round her took it up, and they sang it three times over – very tunefully, but slowly and mournfully, in a way they had never sung it before.

They had just finished singing it for the third time when Squealer, attended by two dogs, approached them with the air of having something important to say. He announced that, by a special decree of Comrade Napoleon, 'Beasts of England' had been abolished. From now onwards it was forbidden to sing it.

The animals were taken aback.

"Why?" cried Muriel.

"It's no longer needed, comrade," said Squealer stiffly. "'Beasts of England' was the song of the Rebellion. But the Rebellion is now completed. The execution of the traitors this afternoon was the final act. The enemy both external and internal has been defeated. In 'Beasts of England' we expressed our longing for a better society in days to come. But that society has now been established. Clearly this song has no longer any purpose."

Frightened though they were, some of the animals might possibly have protested, but at this moment the sheep set up their usual bleating of 'Four legs good, two legs bad', which went on for several minutes and put an end to the discussion.

So 'Beasts of England' was heard no more. In its place Minimus, the poet, had composed another song which began:

Animal Farm, Animal Farm,
Never through me shalt thou come to harm!

and this was sung every Sunday morning after the hoisting of the flag. But somehow neither the words nor the tune ever seemed to the animals to come up to 'Beasts of England'.

substitute replacement

tuneful having a pleasant sound

decree official order

to take aback to be completely surprised

stiff not friendly or relaxed

shalt (*old use*) shall
thou (*old use*) you

to come up to sth. to be as good as sth.

Chapter VIII

to square with sth. to agree with sth.

to meddle in sth. to interfere with sth.

to violate to break

appointed fixed

figure number

retinue *Gefolge*

trumpeter *Trompeter*

to inhabit to live in

to wait upon sb. to serve sb.

Crown Derby late 18th century porcelain

dinner service *Tafelservice*

A few days later, when the terror caused by the executions had died down, some of the animals remembered – or thought they remembered – that the Sixth Commandment decreed "No animal shall kill any other animal." And though no one cared to mention it in the hearing of the pigs or the dogs, it was felt that the killings which had taken place did not square with this. Clover asked Benjamin to read her the Sixth Commandment, and when Benjamin, as usual, said that he refused to meddle in such matters, she fetched Muriel. Muriel read the Commandment for her. It ran: 'No animal shall kill any other animal *without cause*.' Somehow or other, the last two words had slipped out of the animals' memory. But they saw now that the Commandment had not been violated; for clearly there was good reason for killing the traitors who had leagued themselves with Snowball.

Throughout the year the animals worked even harder than they had worked in the previous year. To rebuild the windmill, with walls twice as thick as before, and to finish it by the appointed date, together with the regular work of the farm, was a tremendous labour. There were times when it seemed to the animals that they worked longer hours and fed no better than they had done in Jones's days. On Sunday mornings Squealer, holding down a long strip of paper with his trotter, would read out to them lists of figures proving that the production of every class of foodstuff had increased by two hundred per cent, three hundred per cent, or five hundred per cent, as the case might be. The animals saw no reason to disbelieve him, especially as they could no longer remember very clearly what conditions had been like before the Rebellion. All the same, there were days when they felt that they would sooner have had less figures and more food.

All orders were now issued through Squealer or one of the other pigs. Napoleon himself was not seen in public as often as once in a fortnight. When he did appear, he was attended not only by his retinue of dogs but by a black cockerel who marched in front of him and acted as a kind of trumpeter, letting out a loud 'cock-a-doodle-doo' before Napoleon spoke. Even in the farmhouse, it was said, Napoleon inhabited separate apartments from the others. He took his meals alone, with two dogs to wait upon him, and always ate from the Crown Derby dinner service which had been in the glass cupboard in the drawing-room. It was also announced that the gun would be fired every year on Napoleon's birthday, as well as on the other two anniversaries.

Napoleon was now never spoken of simply as 'Napoleon'. He was always referred to in formal style as 'our Leader, Comrade Napoleon', and the pigs liked to invent for him such titles as Father of All Animals, Terror of Mankind, Protector of the Sheepfold, Ducklings' Friend, and the like. In his speeches, Squealer would talk with the tears rolling down his cheeks of Napoleon's wisdom, the goodness of his heart, and the deep love he bore to all animals everywhere, even and especially the unhappy animals who still lived in ignorance and slavery on other farms. It had become usual to give Napoleon the credit for every successful achievement and every stroke of good fortune. You would often hear one hen remark to another, "Under the guidance of our Leader, Comrade Napoleon, I have laid five eggs in six days"; or two cows, enjoying a drink at the pool, would exclaim, "Thanks to the leadership of Comrade Napoleon, how excellent this water tastes!" The general feeling on the farm was well expressed in a poem entitled 'Comrade Napoleon', which was composed by Minimus and which ran as follows:

Friend of the fatherless!
Fountain of happiness!
Lord of the swill-bucket! Oh, how my soul is on
Fire when I gaze at thy
Calm and commanding eye,
Like the sun in the sky,
Comrade Napoleon!

Thou art the giver of
All that thy creatures love,
Full belly twice a day, clean straw to roll upon;
Every beast great or small
Sleeps at peace in his stall,
Thou watchest over all,
Comrade Napoleon!

Had I a sucking-pig,
Ere he had grown as big
Even as a pint bottle or as a rolling-pin,
He should have learned to be
Faithful and true to thee,
Yes, his first squeak should be
"Comrade Napoleon!"

sheepfold enclosure for sheep
wisdom ability to make good decisions
to bear (bore, borne) to have
stroke of good fortune *Glücksfall*
fountain *here*: a rich source
swill-bucket bucket for food for pigs
thy *(old use)* your
art *(old use)* are
belly *Bauch*
watchest (*old use*) watch
sucking-pig young piglet
ere *(old use)* before
pint unit of measurement for liquids, equals 0.568 litres
rolling-pin *Nudelholz*
thee (*old use*) you

to be surmounted (*fml.*) to have sth. placed higher
to execute to make
through the agency of sb. represented by sb.
negotiation formal discussion to reach an agreement
to skulk to hide
precaution action to prevent a difficult situation; *Vorsichtsmaßnahme*
lest (*fml.*) for fear that
to poison *vergiften*
impending about to happen
to bribe *bestechen*
magistrate sb. with the power to put the law into force; *Richter*
title-deed legal document proving ownership; *Besitzurkunde*
to leak out to let secret information become known
to flog to hit with a whip or stick
furnace *Ofen*
splinter sharp piece of metal, wood or plastic
razor-blade *Rasierklinge*
spur *Sporen*
to clamour to demand sth. loudly
to counsel to advise
rash over-hasty

Napoleon approved of this poem and caused it to be inscribed on the wall of the big barn, at the opposite end from the Seven Commandments. It was surmounted by a portrait of Napoleon, in profile, executed by Squealer in white paint.

Meanwhile, through the agency of Whymper, Napoleon was engaged in complicated negotiations with Frederick and Pilkington. The pile of timber was still unsold. Of the two, Frederick was the more anxious to get hold of it, but he would not offer a reasonable price. At the same time there were renewed rumours that Frederick and his men were plotting to attack Animal Farm and to destroy the windmill, the building of which had aroused furious jealousy in him. Snowball was known to be still skulking on Pinchfield Farm. In the middle of the summer the animals were alarmed to hear that three hens had come forward and confessed that, inspired by Snowball, they had entered into a plot to murder Napoleon. They were executed immediately, and fresh precautions for Napoleon's safety were taken. Four dogs guarded his bed at night, one at each corner, and a young pig named Pinkeye was given the task of tasting all his food before he ate it, lest it should be poisoned.

At about the same time it was given out that Napoleon had arranged to sell the pile of timber to Mr Pilkington; he was also going to enter into a regular agreement for the exchange of certain products between Animal Farm and Foxwood. The relations between Napoleon and Pilkington, though they were only conducted through Whymper, were now almost friendly. The animals distrusted Pilkington as a human being, but greatly preferred him to Frederick whom they both feared and hated. As the summer wore on, and the windmill neared completion, the rumours of an impending treacherous attack grew stronger and stronger. Frederick, it was said, intended to bring against them twenty men all armed with guns, and he had already bribed the magistrates and police, so that if he could once get hold of the title-deeds of Animal Farm they would ask no questions. Moreover, terrible stories were leaking out from Pinchfield about the cruelties that Frederick practised upon his animals. He had flogged an old horse to death, he starved his cows, he had killed a dog by throwing it into the furnace, he amused himself in the evenings by making cocks fight with splinters of razor-blade tied to their spurs. The animals' blood boiled with rage when they heard of these things being done to their comrades, and sometimes they clamoured to be allowed to go out in a body and attack Pinchfield Farm, drive out the humans and set the animals free. But Squealer counselled them to avoid rash actions and trust in Comrade Napoleon's strategy.

Nevertheless, feeling against Frederick continued to run high. One Sunday morning Napoleon appeared in the barn and explained that he had never at any time contemplated selling the pile of timber to Frederick; he considered it beneath his dignity, he said, to have dealings with scoundrels of that description. The pigeons who were still sent out to spread tidings of the Rebellion were forbidden to set foot anywhere on Foxwood, and were also ordered to drop their former slogan of 'Death to Humanity' in favour of 'Death to Frederick'. In the late summer yet another of Snowball's machinations was laid bare. The wheat crop was full of weeds, and it was discovered that on one of his nocturnal visits Snowball had mixed weed seeds with the seed corn. A gander who had been privy to the plot had confessed his guilt to Squealer and immediately committed suicide by swallowing deadly nightshade berries. The animals now also learned that Snowball had never – as many of them had believed hitherto – received the order of 'Animal Hero, First Class'. This was merely a legend which had been spread some time after the Battle of the Cowshed by Snowball himself. So far from being decorated, he had been censured for showing cowardice in the battle. Once again some of the animals heard this with a certain bewilderment, but Squealer was soon able to convince them that their memories had been at fault. In the autumn, by a tremendous, exhausting effort – for the harvest had to be gathered at almost the same time – the windmill was finished. The machinery had still to be installed, and Whymper was negotiating the purchase of it, but the structure was completed. In the teeth of every difficulty, in spite of inexperience, of primitive implements, of bad luck and of Snowball's treachery, the work had been finished punctually to the very day! Tired out but proud, the animals walked round and round their masterpiece, which appeared even more beautiful in their eyes than when it had been built the first time. Moreover, the walls were twice as thick as before. Nothing short of explosives would lay them low this time! And when they thought of how they had laboured, what discouragements they had overcome, and the enormous difference that would be made in their lives when the sails were turning and the dynamos running – when they thought of all this, their tiredness forsook them and they gambolled round and round the windmill, uttering cries of triumph. Napoleon himself, attended by his dogs and his cockerel, came down to inspect the completed work; he personally congratulated the animals on their achievement, and announced that the mill would be named Napoleon Mill.

Two days later the animals were called together for a special meeting in the barn. They were struck dumb with surprise when

to run high to be intense

to contemplate to think about

to have dealings with to be involved with

scoundrel *(old use)* sb. who treats others badly

machination plot; *Machenschaft*

to lay bare to show clearly

gander male goose

privy to sth. familiar with sth.

deadly nightshade poisonous plant; *Schwarze Tollkirsche*

to censure to criticize

cowardice [ˈkaʊədɪs] lack of courage; *Feigheit*

bewilderment confusion

at fault wrong

exhausting tiring

in the teeth of in spite of, faced by

nothing short of almost nothing but

to forsake (forsook, forsaken) to leave

to be struck dumb to be silent with astonishment

Napoleon announced that he had sold the pile of timber to Frederick. Tomorrow Frederick's wagons would arrive and begin carting it away. Throughout the whole period of his seeming friendship with Pilkington, Napoleon had really been in secret agreement with Frederick.

All relations with Foxwood had been broken off; insulting messages had been sent to Pilkington. The pigeons had been told to avoid Pinchfield Farm and to alter their slogan from 'Death to Frederick' to 'Death to Pilkington'. At the same time Napoleon assured the animals that the stories of an impending attack on Animal Farm were completely untrue, and that the tales about Frederick's cruelty to his own animals had been greatly exaggerated. All these rumours had probably originated with Snowball and his agents. It now appeared that Snowball was not, after all, hiding on Pinchfield Farm, and in fact had never been there in his life: he was living – in considerable luxury, so it was said – at Foxwood, and had in reality been a pensioner of Pilkington for years past.

The pigs were in ecstasies over Napoleon's cunning. By seeming to be friendly with Pilkington he had forced Frederick to raise his price by twelve pounds. But the superior quality of Napoleon's mind, said Squealer, was shown in the fact that he trusted nobody, not even Frederick. Frederick had wanted to pay for the timber with something called a cheque, which, it seemed, was a piece of paper with a promise to pay written upon it. But Napoleon was too clever for him. He had demanded payment in real five-pound notes, which were to be handed over before the timber was removed. Already Frederick had paid up; and the sum he had paid was just enough to buy the machinery for the windmill. Meanwhile the timber was being carted away at high speed. When it was all gone, another special meeting was held in the barn for the animals to inspect Frederick's banknotes. Smiling beatifically, and wearing both his decorations, Napoleon reposed on a bed of straw on the platform, with the money at his side, neatly piled on a china dish from the farmhouse kitchen. The animals filed slowly past, and each gazed his fill. And Boxer put out his nose to sniff at the bank-notes, and the flimsy white things stirred and rustled in his breath.

Three days later there was a terrible hullabaloo. Whymper, his face deadly pale, came racing up the path on his bicycle, flung it down in the yard and rushed straight into the farmhouse. The next moment a choking roar of rage sounded from Napoleon's apartments. The news of what had happened sped round the farm like wildfire. The banknotes were forgeries! Frederick had got the timber for nothing!

insulting *beleidigend*

impending that is going to happen very soon

to originate with sb. to be started by sb.

pensioner *Rentner*

beatific (*fml.*) showing great happiness

china porcelain

one's fill as much as one wants

flimsy thin

to rustle to make a soft sound, like dry leaves

hullabaloo uproar

pale white

choking breathless

to speed (sped, sped) to move fast

forgery *Fälschung*

Napoleon called the animals together immediately and in a terrible voice pronounced the death sentence upon Frederick. When captured, he said, Frederick should be boiled alive. At the same time he warned them that after this treacherous deed the worst was to be expected. Frederick and his men might make their long-expected attack at any moment. Sentinels were placed at all the approaches to the farm. In addition, four pigeons were sent to Foxwood with a conciliatory message, which it was hoped might re-establish good relations with Pilkington.

The very next morning the attack came. The animals were at breakfast when the look-outs came racing in with the news that Frederick and his followers had already come through the five-barred gate. Boldly enough the animals sallied forth to meet them, but this time they did not have the easy victory that they had had in the Battle of the Cowshed. There were fifteen men, with half a dozen guns between them, and they opened fire as soon as they got within fifty yards. The animals could not face the terrible explosions and the stinging pellets, and in spite of the efforts of Napoleon and Boxer to rally them, they were soon driven back. A number of them were already wounded. They took refuge in the farm buildings and peeped cautiously out from chinks and knot-holes. The whole of the big pasture, including the windmill, was in the hands of the enemy. For the moment even Napoleon seemed at a loss. He paced up and down without a word, his tail rigid and twitching. Wistful glances were sent in the direction of Foxwood. If Pilkington and his men would help them, the day might yet be won. But at this moment the four pigeons, who had been sent out on the day before, returned, one of them bearing a scrap of paper from Pilkington. On it was pencilled the words: 'Serves you right'.

Meanwhile Frederick and his men had halted about the windmill. The animals watched them, and a murmur of dismay went round. Two of the men had produced a crowbar and a sledge hammer. They were going to knock the windmill down.

"Impossible!" cried Napoleon. "We have built the walls far too thick for that. They could not knock it down in a week. Courage, comrades!"

But Benjamin was watching the movements of the men intently. The two with the hammer and the crowbar were drilling a hole near the base of the windmill. Slowly, and with an air almost of amusement, Benjamin nodded his long muzzle.

"I thought so," he said. "Do you not see what they are doing? In another moment they are going to pack blasting powder into that hole."

Terrified, the animals waited. It was impossible now to venture out of the shelter of the buildings. After a few minutes the men

sentinel guard

conciliatory [kən'sɪliətəri] friendly

look-out sb. who keeps watch

bold confident

to sally forth *(old use)* to leave in a determined way

fifty yards about 45 metres

stinging *stechend*

refuge shelter

to peep to look

chink narrow opening

knot-hole *Astloch*

to pace to walk slowly; *schreiten*

wistful sad

to bear (bore, borne) to carry

dismay feeling of unhappiness

crowbar *Brechstange*

sledge hammer *Vorschlaghammer*

intently very closely

muzzle nose and mouth of an animal

blasting powder explosive powder

to venture ['ventʃər] to risk going somewhere

were seen to be running in all directions. Then there was a deafening roar. The pigeons swirled into the air, and all the animals, except Napoleon, flung themselves flat on their bellies and hid their faces. When they got up again, a huge cloud of black smoke was hanging where the windmill had been. Slowly the breeze drifted it away. The windmill had ceased to exist!

At this sight the animals' courage returned to them. The fear and despair they had felt a moment earlier were drowned in their rage against this vile, contemptible act. A mighty cry for vengeance went up, and without waiting for further orders they charged forth in a body and made straight for the enemy. This time they did not heed the cruel pellets that swept over them like hail. It was a savage, bitter battle. The men fired again and again, and, when the animals got to close quarters, lashed out with their sticks and their heavy boots. A cow, three sheep and two geese were killed, and nearly everyone was wounded. Even Napoleon, who was directing operations from the rear, had the tip of his tail chipped by a pellet. But the men did not go unscathed either. Three of them had their heads broken by blows from Boxer's hoofs; another was gored in the belly by a cow's horn; another had his trousers nearly torn off by Jessie and Bluebell. And when the nine dogs of Napoleon's own bodyguard, whom he had instructed to make a detour under cover of the hedge, suddenly appeared on the men's flank, baying ferociously, panic overtook them. They saw that they were in danger of being surrounded. Frederick shouted to his men to get out while the going was good, and the next moment the cowardly enemy was running for dear life. The animals chased them right down to the bottom of the field, and got in some last kicks at them as they forced their way through the thorn hedge.

They had won, but they were weary and bleeding. Slowly they began to limp back towards the farm. The sight of their dead comrades stretched upon the grass moved some of them to tears. And for a little while they halted in sorrowful silence at the place where the windmill had once stood. Yes, it was gone; almost the last trace of their labour was gone! Even the foundations were partially destroyed. And in rebuilding it they could not this time, as before, make use of the fallen stones. This time the stones had vanished too. The force of the explosion had flung them to distances of hundreds of yards. It was as though the windmill had never been.

As they approached the farm Squealer, who had unaccountably been absent during the fighting, came skipping towards them, whisking his tail and beaming with satisfaction. And the animals heard, from the direction of the farm buildings, the solemn booming of a gun.

deafening *ohrenbetäubend*
to drift to blow
to cease to stop
vile terrible
contemptible (*fml.*) deserving no respect
mighty massive
to heed to notice
savage cruel, violent
to get to close quarters to get very near
unscathed [ʌn'skeɪðd] unharmed
detour *Umweg*
ferocious [fə'rəʊʃəs] aggressive
cowardly not brave
to chase to hunt
weary tired, exhausted
to limp *humpeln*
unaccountable impossible to explain
to beam to have a big smile

"What is that gun firing for?" said Boxer.

"To celebrate our victory!" cried Squealer.

"What victory?" said Boxer. His knees were bleeding, he had lost a shoe and split his hoof, and a dozen pellets had lodged themselves in his hind leg.

"What victory, comrade? Have we not driven the enemy off our soil – the sacred soil of Animal Farm?"

"But they have destroyed the windmill. And we had worked on it for two years!"

"What matter? We will build another windmill. We will build six windmills if we feel like it. You do not appreciate, comrade, the mighty thing that we have done. The enemy was in occupation of this very ground that we stand upon. And now – thanks to the leadership of Comrade Napoleon – we have won every inch of it back again!"

"Then we have won back what we had before," said Boxer.

"That is our victory," said Squealer.

They limped into the yard. The pellets under the skin of Boxer's leg smarted painfully. He saw ahead of him the heavy labour of rebuilding the windmill from the foundations, and already in imagination he braced himself for the task. But for the first time it occurred to him that he was eleven years old and that perhaps his great muscles were not quite what they had once been.

But when the animals saw the green flag flying, and heard the gun firing again – seven times it was fired in all – and heard the speech that Napoleon made, congratulating them on their conduct, it did seem to them after all that they had won a great victory. The animals slain in the battle were given a solemn funeral. Boxer and Clover pulled the wagon which served as a hearse, and Napoleon himself walked at the head of the procession. Two whole days were given over to celebrations. There were songs, speeches and more firing of the gun, and a special gift of an apple was bestowed on every animal, with two ounces of corn for each bird and three biscuits for each dog. It was announced that the battle would be called the Battle of the Windmill, and that Napoleon had created a new decoration, the Order of the Green Banner, which he had conferred upon himself. In the general rejoicings the unfortunate affair of the banknotes was forgotten.

It was a few days later than this that the pigs came upon a case of whisky in the cellars of the farmhouse. It had been overlooked at the time when the house was first occupied. That night there came from the farmhouse the sound of loud singing, in which, to everyone's surprise, the strains of 'Beasts of England' were mixed up. At about half past nine Napoleon, wearing an old bowler hat

to lodge itself *stecken*

in occupation in control

to smart to hurt

to brace oneself to prepare oneself

conduct behaviour

to slay (slain, slain) (*fml.*) to kill

hearse [hɜː(r)s] carriage used to carry a coffin to the grave; *Leichenwagen*

to bestow sth. on sb. to give sb. sth.

two ounces about 57 grams

strains sounds

bowler hat *Melone*

distinct clear

dejected sad and without hope

lamentation loud expression of sadness

to contrive to manage

to purchase to buy

exhausted *ausgelaugt*

to sprawl to lie spread out

of Mr Jones's, was distinctly seen to emerge from the back door, gallop rapidly round the yard, and disappear indoors again. But in the morning a deep silence hung over the farmhouse. Not a pig appeared to be stirring. It was nearly nine o'clock when Squealer made his appearance, walking slowly and dejectedly, his eyes dull, his tail hanging limply behind him, and with every appearance of being seriously ill. He called the animals together and told them that he had a terrible piece of news to impart. Comrade Napoleon was dying!

A cry of lamentation went up. Straw was laid down outside the doors of the farmhouse, and the animals walked on tiptoe. With tears in their eyes they asked one another what they should do if their Leader were taken away from them. A rumour went round that Snowball had after all contrived to introduce poison into Napoleon's food. At eleven o'clock Squealer came out to make another announcement. As his last act upon earth, Comrade Napoleon had pronounced a solemn decree: the drinking of alcohol was to be punished by death.

By the evening, however, Napoleon appeared to be somewhat better, and the following morning Squealer was able to tell them that he was well on the way to recovery. By the evening of that day Napoleon was back at work, and on the next day it was learned that he had instructed Whymper to purchase in Willingdon some booklets on brewing and distilling. A week later Napoleon gave orders that the small paddock beyond the orchard, which it had previously been intended to set aside as a grazing-ground for animals who were past work, was to be ploughed up. It was given out that the pasture was exhausted and needed re-seeding; but it soon became known that Napoleon intended to sow it with barley.

About this time there occurred a strange incident which hardly anyone was able to understand. One night at about twelve o'clock there was a loud crash in the yard, and the animals rushed out of their stalls. It was a moonlit night. At the foot of the end wall of the big barn, where the Seven Commandments were written, there lay a ladder broken in two pieces. Squealer, temporarily stunned, was sprawling beside it, and near at hand there lay a lantern, a paintbrush and an overturned pot of white paint. The dogs immediately made a ring round Squealer, and escorted him back to the farmhouse as soon as he was able to walk. None of the animals could form any idea as to what this meant, except old Benjamin, who nodded his muzzle with a knowing air, and seemed to understand, but would say nothing.

But a few days later Muriel, reading over the Seven Commandments to herself, noticed that there was yet another of them which the animals had remembered wrong. They had thought the Fifth Commandment was 'No animal shall drink alcohol', but there were two words that they had forgotten. Actually the Commandment read: 'No animal shall drink alcohol *to excess*'.

excess more than allowed or proper

Chapter IX

Boxer's split hoof was a long time in healing. They had started the rebuilding of the windmill the day after the victory celebrations were ended. Boxer refused to take even a day off work, and made it a point of honour not to let it be seen that he was in pain. In the evenings he would admit privately to Clover that the hoof troubled him a great deal. Clover treated the hoof with poultices of herbs which she prepared by chewing them, and both she and Benjamin urged Boxer to work less hard. "A horse's lungs do not last for ever," she said to him. But Boxer would not listen. He had, he said, only one real ambition left – to see the windmill well under way before he reached the age for retirement.

poultice *Umschlag, Wickel*
herbs *Kräuter*
to chew to crush food with your teeth
to urge to try hard to persuade sb.

At the beginning, when the laws of Animal Farm were first formulated, the retiring age had been fixed for horses and pigs at twelve, for cows at fourteen, for dogs at nine, for sheep at seven and for hens and geese at five. Liberal old-age pensions had been agreed upon. As yet no animal had actually retired on pension, but of late the subject had been discussed more and more. Now that the small field beyond the orchard had been set aside for barley, it was rumoured that a corner of the large pasture was to be fenced off and turned into a grazing-ground for superannuated animals. For a horse, it was said, the pension would be five pounds of corn a day and, in winter, fifteen pounds of hay, with a carrot or possibly an apple on public holidays. Boxer's twelfth birthday was due in the late summer of the following year.

liberal *here*: generous
superannuated (*fml.*) too old for work
five pounds 2.25 kg

Meanwhile life was hard. The winter was as cold as the last one had been, and food was even shorter. Once again all rations were reduced, except those of the pigs and the dogs. A too rigid equality in rations, Squealer explained, would have been contrary to the principles of Animalism. In any case he had no difficulty in proving to the other animals that they were *not* in reality short of food, whatever the appearances might be. For the time being, certainly, it had been found necessary to make a readjustment of rations (Squealer always spoke of it as a 'readjustment', never as a 'reduction'), but in comparison with the days of Jones, the improvement was enormous. Reading out the figures in a shrill, rapid voice, he proved to them in detail that they had more oats, more hay, more turnips than they had had in Jones's day, that they worked shorter hours, that their drinking water was of better quality, that they lived longer, that a larger proportion of their young ones survived infancy, and that they had more straw in their stalls and suffered less from fleas. The animals believed every word of it. Truth to tell, Jones and all he stood for had al-

rigid strict
readjustment new arrangement
fleas *Flöhe*

most faded out of their memories. They knew that life nowadays was harsh and bare, that they were often hungry and often cold, and that they were usually working when they were not asleep. But doubtless it had been worse in the old days. They were glad to believe so. Besides, in those days they had been slaves and now they were free, and that made all the difference, as Squealer did not fail to point out.

There were many more mouths to feed now. In the autumn the four sows had all littered about simultaneously, producing thirty-one young pigs between them. The young pigs were piebald, and as Napoleon was the only boar on the farm, it was possible to guess at their parentage. It was announced that later, when bricks and timber had been purchased, a schoolroom would be built in the farmhouse garden. For the time being, the young pigs were given their instruction by Napoleon himself in the farmhouse kitchen. They took their exercise in the garden, and were discouraged from playing with the other young animals. About this time, too, it was laid down as a rule that when a pig and any other animal met on the path, the other animal must stand aside: and also that all pigs, of whatever degree, were to have the privilege of wearing green ribbons on their tails on Sundays.

The farm had had a fairly successful year, but was still short of money. There were the bricks, sand and lime for the schoolroom to be purchased, and it would also be necessary to begin saving up again for the machinery for the windmill. Then there were lamp oil and candles for the house, sugar for Napoleon's own table (he forbade this to the other pigs, on the ground that it made them fat), and all the usual replacements such as tools, nails, string, coal, wire, scrap-iron and dog biscuits. A stump of hay and part of the potato crop were sold off, and the contract for eggs was increased to six hundred a week, so that that year the hens barely hatched enough chicks to keep their numbers at the same level. Rations, reduced in December, were reduced again in February, and lanterns in the stalls were forbidden to save oil. But the pigs seemed comfortable enough, and in fact were putting on weight if anything. One afternoon in late February a warm, rich, appetizing scent, such as the animals had never smelt before, wafted itself across the yard from the little brew-house, which had been disused in Jones's time, and which stood beyond the kitchen. Someone said it was the smell of cooking barley. The animals sniffed the air hungrily and wondered whether a warm mash was being prepared for their supper. But no warm mash appeared, and on the following Sunday it was announced that from now onwards all barley would be reserved for the pigs. The field beyond the orchard had already been sown

bare with hardly enough

to litter to have babies (only animals)
piebald two-coloured

scrap-iron *Schrott*
stump of hay remains of a stack (*Stapel*)

barely hardly
to hatch *(aus)brüten*

scent *Duft*

to waft [wɒft] to blow gently
brew-house *Brauhaus*

with barley. And the news soon leaked out that every pig was now receiving a ration of a pint of beer daily, with half a gallon for Napoleon himself, which was always served to him in the Crown Derby soup tureen.

But if there were hardships to be borne, they were partly offset by the fact that life nowadays had a greater dignity than it had had before. There were more songs, more speeches, more processions. Napoleon had commanded that once a week there should be held something called a Spontaneous Demonstration, the object of which was to celebrate the struggles and triumphs of Animal Farm. At the appointed time the animals would leave their work and march round the precincts of the farm in military formation, with the pigs leading, then the horses, then the cows, then the sheep, and then the poultry. The dogs flanked the procession and at the head of all marched Napoleon's black cockerel. Boxer and Clover always carried between them a green banner marked with the hoof and the horn and the caption, 'Long live Comrade Napoleon!' Afterwards there were recitations of poems composed in Napoleon's honour, and a speech by Squealer giving particulars of the latest increases in the production of foodstuffs, and on occasion a shot was fired from the gun. The sheep were the greatest devotees of the Spontaneous Demonstrations, and if anyone complained (as a few animals sometimes did, when no pigs or dogs were near) that they wasted time and meant a lot of standing about in the cold, the sheep were sure to silence him with a tremendous bleating of 'Four legs good, two legs bad!' But by and large the animals enjoyed these celebrations. They found it comforting to be reminded that, after all, they were truly their own masters and that the work they did was for their own benefit. So that, what with the songs, the processions, Squealer's lists of figures, the thunder of the gun, the crowing of the cockerel and the fluttering of the flag, they were able to forget that their bellies were empty, at least part of the time.

In April Animal Farm was proclaimed a Republic, and it became necessary to elect a President. There was only one candidate, Napoleon, who was elected unanimously. On the same day it was given out that fresh documents had been discovered which revealed further details about Snowball's complicity with Jones. It now appeared that Snowball had not, as the animals had previously imagined, merely attempted to lose the Battle of the Cowshed by means of a stratagem, but had been openly fighting on Jones's side. In fact, it was he who had actually been the leader of the human forces, and had charged into battle with the words 'Long live Humanity!' on his lips. The wounds on Snowball's

tureen *Terrine*
hardship difficult situation
to offset (offset, offset) to balance
precinct outer limits
poultry chicken, geese, ducks
caption words underneath a picture
particulars details
devotee fan, supporter
by and large generally
to proclaim to officially declare
unanimous [juːˈnænɪməs] with the votes of everybody
complicity partnership in crime
stratagem trick

back, which a few of the animals still remembered to have seen, had been inflicted by Napoleon's teeth.

In the middle of the summer Moses the raven suddenly reappeared on the farm, after an absence of several years. He was quite unchanged, still did no work, and talked in the same strain as ever about Sugarcandy Mountain. He would perch on a stump, flap his black wings, and talk by the hour to anyone who would listen. "Up there, comrades," he would say solemnly, pointing to the sky with his large beak – "up there, just on the other side of that dark cloud that you can see – there it lies, Sugarcandy Mountain, that happy country where we poor animals shall rest for ever from our labours!" He even claimed to have been there on one of his higher flights, and to have seen the everlasting fields of clover and the linseed cake and lump sugar growing on the hedges. Many of the animals believed him. Their lives now, they reasoned, were hungry and laborious; was it not right and just that a better world should exist somewhere else? A thing that was difficult to determine was the attitude of the pigs towards Moses. They all declared contemptuously that his stories about Sugarcandy Mountain were lies, and yet they allowed him to remain on the farm, not working, with an allowance of a gill of beer a day.

After his hoof had healed up, Boxer worked harder than ever. Indeed, all the animals worked like slaves that year. Apart from the regular work of the farm, and the rebuilding of the windmill, there was the schoolhouse for the young pigs, which was started in March. Sometimes the long hours on insufficient food were hard to bear, but Boxer never faltered. In nothing that he said or did was there any sign that his strength was not what it had been. It was only his appearance that was a little altered; his hide was less shiny than it had used to be, and his great haunches seemed to have shrunken. The others said, "Boxer will pick up when the spring grass comes on"; but the spring grass came and Boxer grew no fatter. Sometimes on the slope leading to the top of the quarry, when he braced his muscles against the weight of some vast boulder, it seemed that nothing kept him on his feet except the will to continue. At such times his lips were seen to form the words, "I will work harder"; he had no voice left. Once again Clover and Benjamin warned him to take care of his health, but Boxer paid no attention. His twelfth birthday was approaching. He did not care what happened so long as a good store of stone was accumulated before he went on pension.

Late one evening in the summer, a sudden rumour ran round the farm that something had happened to Boxer. He had gone out alone to drag a load of stone down to the windmill. And sure enough, the rumour was true. A few minutes later two pigeons

to inflict to cause

strain way

to reason to argue

contemptuous [kənˈtemptʃuəsli] with no respect
allowance *Ration*
gill [gɪl] ¼ pint

to falter to become weaker

hide skin and fur

haunch *Lende*

to have shrunken to have become smaller

to brace against sth. to press hard against sth.

to accumulate [əˈkjuːmjəleɪt] to collect

came racing in with the news: "Boxer has fallen! He is lying on his side and can't get up!"

About half the animals on the farm rushed out to the knoll where the windmill stood. There lay Boxer, between the shafts of the cart, his neck stretched out, unable even to raise his head. His eyes were glazed, his sides matted with sweat. A thin stream of blood had trickled out of his mouth. Clover dropped to her knees at his side.

to trickle to pass in a thin stream; *tropfen*

"Boxer!" she cried, "how are you?"

"It is my lung," said Boxer in a weak voice. "It does not matter. I think you will be able to finish the windmill without me. There is a pretty good store of stone accumulated. I had only another month to go in any case. To tell you the truth, I had been looking forward to my retirement. And perhaps, as Benjamin is growing old too, they will let him retire at the same time and be a companion to me."

"We must get help at once," said Clover. "Run, somebody, and tell Squealer what has happened."

All the other animals immediately raced back to the farmhouse to give Squealer the news. Only Clover remained, and Benjamin, who lay down at Boxer's side, and, without speaking, kept the flies off him with his long tail. After about a quarter of an hour Squealer appeared, full of sympathy and concern. He said that Comrade Napoleon had learned with the very deepest distress of this misfortune to one of the most loyal workers on the farm, and was already making arrangements to send Boxer to be treated in the hospital at Willingdon. The animals felt a little uneasy at this. Except for Mollie and Snowball, no other animal had ever left the farm, and they did not like to think of their sick comrade in the hands of human beings. However, Squealer easily convinced them that the veterinary surgeon in Willingdon could treat Boxer's case more satisfactorily than could be done on the farm. And about half an hour later, when Boxer had somewhat recovered, he was with difficulty got on to his feet, and managed to limp back to his stall, where Clover and Benjamin had prepared a good bed of straw for him.

distress worry, sadness, pain

veterinary surgeon *Tierarzt*

For the next two days Boxer remained in his stall. The pigs had sent out a large bottle of pink medicine which they had found in the medicine chest in the bathroom, and Clover administered it to Boxer twice a day after meals. In the evenings she lay in his stall and talked to him, while Benjamin kept the flies off him. Boxer professed not to be sorry for what had happened. If he made a good recovery, he might expect to live another three years, and he looked forward to the peaceful days that he would spend in the corner of the big pasture. It would be the first time

to profess (*fml.*) to declare

that he had had leisure to study and improve his mind. He intended, he said, to devote the rest of his life to learning the remaining twenty-two letters of the alphabet.

to devote to sth. to spend

However, Benjamin and Clover could only be with Boxer after working hours, and it was in the middle of the day when the van came to take him away. The animals were all at work weeding turnips under the supervision of a pig, when they were astonished to see Benjamin come galloping from the direction of the farm buildings, braying at the top of his voice. It was the first time that they had ever seen Benjamin excited – indeed, it was the first time that anyone had ever seen him gallop. "Quick, quick!" he shouted. "Come at once! They're taking Boxer away!"

Without waiting for orders from the pig, the animals broke off work and raced back to the farm buildings. Sure enough, there in the yard was a large closed van, drawn by two horses, with lettering on its side and a sly-looking man in a low-crowned bowler hat sitting on the driver's seat. And Boxer's stall was empty.

low-crowned rather flat

The animals crowded round the van. "Good-bye, Boxer!" they chorused, "good-bye!"

to chorus to say together

"Fools! Fools!" shouted Benjamin, prancing round them and stamping the earth with his small hoofs. "Fools! Do you not see what is written on the side of that van?"

That gave the animals pause, and there was a hush. Muriel began to spell out the words. But Benjamin pushed her aside and in the midst of a deadly silence he read:

hush moment of silence

"'Alfred Simmonds, Horse Slaughterer and Glue Boiler, Willingdon. Dealer in Hides and Bone-Meal. Kennels Supplied.' Do you not understand what that means? They are taking Boxer to the knacker's!"

slaughterer butcher
glue boiler *Leimhersteller*
bone-meal *Knochenmehl*
kennel dog hut

A cry of horror burst from all the animals. At this moment the man on the box whipped up his horses and the van moved out of the yard at a smart trot. All the animals followed, crying out at the tops of their voices. Clover forced her way to the front. The van began to gather speed. Clover tried to stir her stout limbs to a gallop, and achieved a canter. "Boxer!" she cried. "Boxer! Boxer! Boxer!" And just at this moment, as though he had heard the uproar outside, Boxer's face, with the white stripe down his nose, appeared at the small window at the back of the van.

box *Kutschbock*
smart quick
canter *leichter Galopp*

"Boxer!" cried Clover in a terrible voice. "Boxer! Get out! Get out quickly! They're taking you to your death!"

All the animals took up the cry of "Get out, Boxer, get out!" But the van was already gathering speed and drawing away from them. It was uncertain whether Boxer had understood what Clover had said. But a moment later his face disappeared from the window and there was the sound of a tremendous drumming

matchwood very small piece of wood; *Späne*
alas (*old use*) expression of sadness
brute *Tier*
affecting moving, emotional
demeanour behaviour and appearance
to dart to move quickly
suspicious feeling like sth. or sb. cannot be trusted; *misstrauisch*
indignant angry
to arise to come about
relieved *erleichtert*

of hoofs inside the van. He was trying to kick his way out. The time had been when a few kicks from Boxer's hoofs would have smashed the van to matchwood. But alas! His strength had left him; and in a few moments the sound of drumming hoofs grew fainter and died away. In desperation the animals began appealing to the two horses which drew the van to stop. "Comrades, comrades!" they shouted.

"Don't take your own brother to his death!" But the stupid brutes, too ignorant to realize what was happening, merely set back their ears and quickened their pace. Boxer's face did not reappear at the window. Too late, someone thought of racing ahead and shutting the five-barred gate; but in another moment the van was through it and rapidly disappearing down the road. Boxer was never seen again.

Three days later it was announced that he had died in the hospital at Willingdon, in spite of receiving every attention a horse could have. Squealer came to announce the news to the others. He had, he said, been present during Boxer's last hours.

"It was the most affecting sight I have ever seen!" said Squealer, lifting his trotter and wiping away a tear. "I was at his bedside at the very last. And at the end, almost too weak to speak, he whispered in my ear that his sole sorrow was to have passed on before the windmill was finished. 'Forward, comrades!' he whispered. 'Forward in the name of the Rebellion. Long live Animal Farm! Long live Comrade Napoleon! Napoleon is always right.' Those were his very last words, comrades."

Here Squealer's demeanour suddenly changed. He fell silent for a moment, and his little eyes darted suspicious glances from side to side before he proceeded.

It had come to his knowledge, he said, that a foolish and wicked rumour had been circulated at the time of Boxer's removal. Some of the animals had noticed that the van which took Boxer away was marked 'Horse Slaughterer', and had actually jumped to the conclusion that Boxer was being sent to the knacker's. It was almost unbelievable, said Squealer, that any animal could be so stupid. Surely, he cried indignantly, whisking his tail and skipping from side to side, surely they knew their beloved Leader, Comrade Napoleon, better than that? But the explanation was really very simple. The van had previously been the property of the knacker, and had been bought by the veterinary surgeon, who had not yet painted the old name out. That was how the mistake had arisen.

The animals were enormously relieved to hear this. And when Squealer went on to give further graphic details of Boxer's deathbed, the admirable care he had received, and the expensive medicines for which Napoleon had paid without a thought as to the cost, their last doubts disappeared and the sorrow that they felt for their comrade's death was tempered by the thought that at least he had died happy.

Napoleon himself appeared at the meeting on the following Sunday morning and pronounced a short oration in Boxer's honour. It had not been possible, he said, to bring back their lamented comrade's remains for interment on the farm, but he had ordered a large wreath to be made from the laurels in the farmhouse garden and sent down to be placed on Boxer's grave. And in a few days' time the pigs intended to hold a memorial banquet in Boxer's honour. Napoleon ended his speech with a reminder of Boxer's two favourite maxims, "I will work harder" and "Comrade Napoleon is always right"–maxims, he said, which every animal would do well to adopt as his own.

On the day appointed for the banquet, a grocer's van drove up from Willingdon and delivered a large wooden crate at the farmhouse. That night there was the sound of uproarious singing, which was followed by what sounded like a violent quarrel and ended at about eleven o'clock with a tremendous crash of glass. No one stirred in the farmhouse before noon on the following day, and the word went round that from somewhere or other the pigs had acquired the money to buy themselves another case of whisky.

oration (*fml.*) speech

interment (*fml.*) burial

wreath [ri:θ] *Kranz*

laurel *Lorbeer*

crate box

uproarious extremely loud

to acquire (*fml.*) to get

Chapter X

to pass to go by

to flee (fled, fled) **by** to pass quickly

inebriate [ɪˈniːbriət] alcoholic

joint *Gelenk*

rheumy watery

twenty-four stone over 152 kg

morose in a bad mood

taciturn quiet

dim vague, distant

by word of mouth by people telling sth.

upstanding honest

filial child-like

prosperous wealthy

hay elevator *Getreideheber*

Years passed. The seasons came and went, the short animal lives fled by. A time came when there was no one who remembered the old days before the Rebellion, except Clover, Benjamin, Moses the raven, and a number of the pigs.

Muriel was dead; Bluebell, Jessie and Pincher were dead. Jones too was dead – he had died in an inebriates' home in another part of the county. Snowball was forgotten. Boxer was forgotten, except by the few who had known him. Clover was an old stout mare now, stiff in the joints and with a tendency to rheumy eyes. She was two years past the retiring age, but in fact no animal had ever actually retired. The talk of setting aside a corner of the pasture for superannuated animals had long since been dropped. Napoleon was now a mature boar of twenty-four stone. Squealer was so fat that he could with difficulty see out of his eyes. Only old Benjamin was much the same as ever, except for being a little greyer about the muzzle, and, since Boxer's death, more morose and taciturn than ever.

There were many more creatures on the farm now, though the increase was not so great as had been expected in earlier years. Many animals had been born to whom the Rebellion was only a dim tradition, passed on by word of mouth, and others had been bought who had never heard mention of such a thing before their arrival. The farm possessed three horses now besides Clover. They were fine upstanding beasts, willing workers and good comrades, but very stupid. None of them proved able to learn the alphabet beyond the letter B. They accepted everything that they were told about the Rebellion and the principles of Animalism, especially from Clover, for whom they had an almost filial respect; but it was doubtful whether they understood very much of it.

The farm was more prosperous now, and better organized; it had even been enlarged by two fields which had been bought from Mr Pilkington. The windmill had been successfully completed at last, and the farm possessed a threshing machine and a hay elevator of its own, and various new buildings had been added to it. Whymper had bought himself a dogcart. The windmill, however, had not after all been used for generating electrical power. It was used for milling corn, and brought in a handsome money profit. The animals were hard at work building yet another windmill; when that one was finished, so it was said, the dynamos would be installed. But the luxuries of which Snowball had once taught the animals to dream, the stalls with electric light and hot and cold water, and the three-day week, were no longer talked about.

Napoleon had denounced such ideas as contrary to the spirit of Animalism. The truest happiness, he said, lay in working hard and living frugally.

Somehow it seemed as though the farm had grown richer without making the animals themselves any richer – except, of course, for the pigs and the dogs. Perhaps this was partly because there were so many pigs and so many dogs. It was not that these creatures did not work, after their fashion. There was, as Squealer was never tired of explaining, endless work in the supervision and organization of the farm. Much of this work was of a kind that the other animals were too ignorant to understand. For example, Squealer told them that the pigs had to expend enormous labours every day upon mysterious things called 'files', 'reports', 'minutes' and 'memoranda'. These were large sheets of paper which had to be closely covered with writing, and as soon as they were so covered, they were burnt in the furnace. This was of the highest importance for the welfare of the farm, Squealer said. But still, neither pigs nor dogs produced any food by their own labour; and there were very many of them, and their appetites were always good.

As for the others, their life, so far as they knew, was as it had always been. They were generally hungry, they slept on straw, they drank from the pool, they laboured in the fields; in winter they were troubled by the cold, and in summer by the flies. Sometimes the older ones among them racked their dim memories and tried to determine whether in the early days of the Rebellion, when Jones's expulsion was still recent, things had been better or worse than now. They could not remember. There was nothing with which they could compare their present lives: they had nothing to go upon except Squealer's lists of figures, which invariably demonstrated that everything was getting better and better. The animals found the problem insoluble; in any case, they had little time for speculating on such things now. Only old Benjamin professed to remember every detail of his long life and to know that things never had been, nor ever could be much better or much worse – hunger, hardship and disappointment being, so he said, the unalterable law of life.

And yet the animals never gave up hope. More, they never lost, even for an instant, their sense of honour and privilege in being members of Animal Farm. They were still the only farm in the whole county – in all England! – owned and operated by animals. Not one of them, not even the youngest, not even the newcomers who had been brought from farms ten or twenty miles away, ever ceased to marvel at that. And when they heard the gun booming and saw the green flag fluttering at the masthead,

to denounce to criticize strongly

frugal *sparsam*

to expend to use up

minute (written) record of a meeting; *Protokoll*

memoranda (*pl.*) notes on legal agreements

to rack one's memory to think very hard

insoluble without a solution

unalterable unchangeable

imperishable (*fml.*) never ending

to abandon to give up

untrodden not stepped or walked on

birch *Birke*

sapling young tree

to browse to feed on

to neigh *wiehern*

to stop in one's tracks to come to an immediate halt

bulk large size

a trifle slightly

their hearts swelled with imperishable pride, and the talk turned always towards the old heroic days, the expulsion of Jones, the writing of the Seven Commandments, the great battles in which the human invaders had been defeated. None of the old dreams had been abandoned. The Republic of the Animals which Major had foretold, when the green fields of England should be untrodden by human feet, was still believed in. Some day it was coming: it might not be soon, it might not be within the lifetime of any animal now living, but still it was coming. Even the tune of 'Beasts of England' was perhaps hummed secretly here and there: at any rate, it was a fact that every animal on the farm knew it, though no one would have dared to sing it aloud. It might be that their lives were hard and that not all of their hopes had been fulfilled; but they were conscious that they were not as other animals. If they went hungry, it was not from feeding tyrannical human beings; if they worked hard, at least they worked for themselves. No creature among them went upon two legs. No creature called any other creature 'Master'. All animals were equal.

One day in early summer Squealer ordered the sheep to follow him and led them out to a piece of waste ground at the other end of the farm, which had become overgrown with birch saplings. The sheep spent the whole day there browsing at the leaves under Squealer's supervision. In the evening he returned to the farmhouse himself, but, as it was warm weather, told the sheep to stay where they were. It ended by their remaining there for a whole week, during which time the other animals saw nothing of them. Squealer was with them for the greater part of every day. He was, he said, teaching them to sing a new song, for which privacy was needed.

It was just after the sheep had returned, on a pleasant evening when the animals had finished work and were making their way back to the farm buildings, that the terrified neighing of a horse sounded from the yard. Startled, the animals stopped in their tracks. It was Clover's voice. She neighed again, and all the animals broke into a gallop and rushed into the yard. Then they saw what Clover had seen.

It was a pig walking on his hind legs.

Yes, it was Squealer. A little awkwardly, as though not quite used to supporting his considerable bulk in that position, but with perfect balance, he was strolling across the yard. And, a moment later, out from the door of the farmhouse came a long file of pigs, all walking on their hind legs. Some did it better than others, one or two were even a trifle unsteady and looked as though they would have liked the support of a stick, but every one of them made his way right round the yard successfully. And finally there was a tremendous baying of dogs and a shrill crowing from the black cockerel, and out came Napoleon himself, majestically upright, casting haughty glances from side to side, and with his dogs gambolling round him.

He carried a whip in his trotter.

There was a deadly silence. Amazed, terrified, huddling together, the animals watched the long line of pigs march slowly round the yard. It was as though the world had turned upside-down. Then there came a moment when the first shock had worn off and when, in spite of everything – in spite of their terror of the dogs, and of the habit, developed through long years, of never complaining, never criticizing, no matter what happened – they might have uttered some word of protest. But just at that moment, as though at a signal, all the sheep burst out into a tremendous bleating of – 'Four legs good, two legs *better*! Four legs good, two legs *better*! Four legs good, two legs *better*!'

It went on for five minutes without stopping. And by the time the sheep had quieted down, the chance to utter any protest had passed, for the pigs had marched back into the farmhouse.

Benjamin felt a nose nuzzling at his shoulder. He looked round. It was Clover. Her old eyes looked dimmer than ever. Without saying anything, she tugged gently at his mane and led him round to the end of the big barn, where the Seven Commandments were written. For a minute or two they stood gazing at the tarred wall with its white lettering.

"My sight is failing," she said finally. "Even when I was young I could not have read what was written there. But it appears to me that that wall looks different. Are the Seven Commandments the same as they used to be, Benjamin?"

For once Benjamin consented to break his rule, and he read out to her what was written on the wall. There was nothing there now except a single Commandment. It ran:

ALL ANIMALS ARE EQUAL
BUT SOME ANIMALS ARE MORE EQUAL THAN OTHERS.

After that it did not seem strange when next day the pigs who were supervising the work of the farm all carried whips in their trotters. It did not seem strange to learn that the pigs had bought themselves a wireless set, were arranging to install a telephone, and had taken out subscriptions to *John Bull*, *Tit-Bits* and the *Daily Mirror*. It did not seem strange when Napoleon was seen strolling in the farmhouse garden with a pipe in his mouth – no, not even when the pigs took Mr Jones's clothes out of the ward-

haughty [ˈhɔ:ti] arrogant

to nuzzle to touch sb. with the nose or face

to tug to pull

to consent to agree

wireless set radio

subscription *Abonnement*

John Bull, Tit-Bits, Daily Mirror tabloid magazines and newspapers

ratcatcher breeches leather trousers that do not cover the whole leg
watered silk special style of silk
diligent steady and tireless
to mingle to mix
stricken with filled with an unpleasant feeling of sth.
eminent important
seat of honour special seat
at ease relaxed
evidently apparently
jug *Krug*
to circulate to be passed from one person to another
mug *Becher*
incumbent upon sb. (*fml.*) sb.'s duty
sentiment thought, opinion
proprietor owner
regarded seen
hostility angry opposition
misgiving feeling of doubt or worry
current *in Umlauf*
to assume to think that sth. is true
due proper
enquiry process of finding out the truth

robes and put them on, Napoleon himself appearing in a black coat, ratcatcher breeches and leather leggings, while his favourite sow appeared in the watered silk dress which Mrs Jones had been used to wear on Sundays.

A week later, in the afternoon, a number of dogcarts drove up to the farm. A deputation of neighbouring farmers had been invited to make a tour of inspection. They were shown all over the farm, and expressed great admiration for everything they saw, especially the windmill. The animals were weeding the turnip field. They worked diligently, hardly raising their faces from the ground, and not knowing whether to be more frightened of the pigs or of the human visitors.

That evening loud laughter and bursts of singing came from the farmhouse. And suddenly, at the sound of the mingled voices, the animals were stricken with curiosity. What could be happening in there, now that for the first time animals and human beings were meeting on terms of equality? With one accord they began to creep as quietly as possible into the farmhouse garden. At the gate they paused, half frightened to go on, but Clover led the way in. They tiptoed up to the house, and such animals as were tall enough peered in at the dining-room window. There, round the long table, sat half a dozen farmers and half a dozen of the more eminent pigs, Napoleon himself occupying the seat of honour at the head of the table. The pigs appeared completely at ease in their chairs. The company had been enjoying a game of cards, but had broken off for the moment, evidently in order to drink a toast. A large jug was circulating, and the mugs were being refilled with beer. No one noticed the wondering faces of the animals that gazed in at the window.

Mr Pilkington, of Foxwood, had stood up, his mug in his hand. In a moment, he said, he would ask the present company to drink a toast. But before doing so, there were a few words that he felt it incumbent upon him to say.

It was a source of great satisfaction to him, he said – and, he was sure, to all others present – to feel that a long period of mistrust and misunderstanding had now come to an end. There had been a time – not that he, or any of the present company, had shared such sentiments – but there had been a time when the respected proprietors of Animal Farm had been regarded, he would not say with hostility, but perhaps with a certain measure of misgiving, by their human neighbours. Unfortunate incidents had occurred, mistaken ideas had been current. It had been felt that the existence of a farm owned and operated by pigs was somehow abnormal and was liable to have an unsettling effect in the neighbourhood. Too many farmers had assumed, without due enquiry, that on such a farm a spirit of licence and indiscipline would prevail. They had been nervous about the effects upon their own animals, or even upon their human employees. But all such doubts were now dispelled. Today he and his friends had visited Animal Farm and inspected every inch of it with their own eyes, and what did they find? Not only the most up-to-date methods, but a discipline and an orderliness which should be an example to all farmers everywhere. He believed that he was right in saying that the lower animals on Animal Farm did more work and received less food than any animals in the county. Indeed, he and his fellow-visitors today had observed many features which they intended to introduce on their own farms immediately.

He would end his remarks, he said, by emphasizing once again the friendly feelings that subsisted, and ought to subsist, between Animal Farm and its neighbours. Between pigs and human beings there was not, and there need not be, any clash of interests whatever. Their struggles and their difficulties were one. Was not the labour problem the same everywhere? Here it became apparent that Mr Pilkington was about to spring some carefully prepared witticism on the company, but for a moment he was too overcome by amusement to be able to utter it. After much choking, during which his various chins turned purple, he managed to get it out: "If you have your lower animals to contend with," he said, "we have our lower classes!" This *bon mot* set the table in a roar; and Mr Pilkington once again congratulated the pigs on the low rations, the long working hours and the general absence of pampering which he had observed on Animal Farm.

And now, he said finally, he would ask the company to rise to their feet and make certain that their glasses were full. "Gentlemen," concluded Mr Pilkington, "gentlemen, I give you a toast: To the prosperity of Animal Farm!"

There was enthusiastic cheering and stamping of feet. Napoleon was so gratified that he left his place and came round the table to clink his mug against Mr Pilkington's before emptying it. When the cheering had died down, Napoleon, who had remained on his feet, intimated that he too had a few words to say.

Like all of Napoleon's speeches, it was short and to the point. He too, he said, was happy that the period of misunderstanding was at an end. For a long time there had been rumours – circulated, he had reason to think, by some malignant enemy – that there was something subversive and even revolutionary in the outlook of himself and his colleagues. They had been credited with attempting to stir up rebellion among the animals on neighbouring farms. Nothing could be further from the truth! Their sole wish, now and in the past, was to live at peace and in normal

licence lack of rules; *Zügellosigkeit*
to prevail *herrschen*
to dispel to remove
to emphasize to stress the importance of sth.
to subsist to exist
clash conflict
whatever at all
witticism clever remark
to contend with to deal with
bon mot funny and clever remark
to pamper to treat very well
to gratify to please, to satisfy
to clink *anstoßen*
to intimate (*fml.*) to let it be known
malignant showing a strong desire to harm sb.
subversive destructive
to be credited with to be held responsible for
sole only

jointly collectively
suspicion *Argwohn*
to linger to continue to exist
to promote to help sth. to develop
to suppress to stop
henceforward (*fml.*) from this time on
dregs the last drops
to flit to move quickly
quarrel angry argument
denial claim that sth. is not true
ace of spades *Pik-As*

business relations with their neighbours. This farm which he had the honour to control, he added, was a co-operative enterprise. The title-deeds, which were in his own possession, were owned by the pigs jointly.

He did not believe, he said, that any of the old suspicions still lingered, but certain changes had been made recently in the routine of the farm which should have the effect of promoting confidence still further. Hitherto the animals on the farm had had a rather foolish custom of addressing one another as 'Comrade'. This was to be suppressed. There had also been a very strange custom, whose origin was unknown, of marching every Sunday morning past a boar's skull which was nailed to a post in the garden. This, too, would be suppressed, and the skull had already been buried. His visitors might have observed, too, the green flag which flew from the masthead. If so, they would perhaps have noted that the white hoof and horn with which it had previously been marked had now been removed. It would be a plain green flag from now onwards.

He had only one criticism, he said, to make of Mr Pilkington's excellent and neighbourly speech. Mr Pilkington had referred throughout to 'Animal Farm'. He could not of course know – for he, Napoleon, was only now for the first time announcing it – that the name "Animal Farm" had been abolished. Henceforward the farm was to be known as 'The Manor Farm' – which, he believed, was its correct and original name.

"Gentlemen," concluded Napoleon, "I will give you the same toast as before, but in a different form. Fill your glasses to the brim. Gentlemen, here is my toast: To the prosperity of The Manor Farm!"

There was the same hearty cheering as before, and the mugs were emptied to the dregs. But as the animals outside gazed at the scene, it seemed to them that some strange thing was happening. What was it that had altered in the faces of the pigs? Clover's old dim eyes flitted from one face to another. Some of them had five chins, some had four, some had three. But what was it that seemed to be melting and changing? Then, the applause having come to an end, the company took up their cards and continued the game that had been interrupted, and the animals crept silently away.

But they had not gone twenty yards when they stopped short. An uproar of voices was coming from the farmhouse. They rushed back and looked through the window again. Yes, a violent quarrel was in progress. There were shoutings, bangings on the table, sharp suspicious glances, furious denials. The source of the trouble appeared to be that Napoleon and Mr Pilkington had each played an ace of spades simultaneously.

Twelve voices were shouting in anger, and they were all alike. No question, now, what had happened to the faces of the pigs. The creatures outside looked from pig to man, and from man to pig, and from pig to man again; but already it was impossible to say which was which.

November 1943 – February 1944

Additional texts

About the Author – George Orwell

George Orwell was born Eric Blair on 25 January 1903 in India. His father was a British colonial civil servant but Blair, his older sister and mother returned to Britain when he was four, while their father remained in India for another five years.

Blair was educated as a public school scholarship student as his family belonged to the middle-class and were not very wealthy. Blair felt like he never fitted in and hated his school years. He soon discovered his passion for writing but decided against going to college after graduating from Eton. Instead, he went to Burma and joined the Indian Imperial Police.

His dislike for both the political system he had to work for as well as the methods used by the police, caused him to return to Europe after only five years. Inspired by the author Jack London, he chose to live in very poor conditions in London and Paris for a while and published his experiences in *Down and Out in Paris and London* in 1933. In order to protect his family from any embarrassment, he used his pen-name George Orwell for the first time. The following year, he published *Burmese Days*, in which he reflected on his time in Burma and criticized British colonialism and imperialism in general.

In 1936, Orwell married Eileen O'Shaughnessy and moved to Hertfordshire. He became more interested in socialism and at the end of the same year travelled to Spain to cover the Spanish Civil War. While at first he was so enthusiastic about socialism that he even took part in the fight for it, he soon realized its limits and that there would always be a class divide. That made him a harsh critic of communism.

In 1938, he was diagnosed with tuberculosis and was consequently rejected from becoming involved in the war effort at the outset of the Second World War. Instead, he worked as a journalist and later focused on writing his novel *Animal Farm*, in which he criticized the Soviet Communist Party and Joseph Stalin.

Orwell and his wife adopted a son, but unfortunately his wife died a year later, in 1945, while undergoing surgery. A year later, he moved to the island of Jura in Scotland and published what many consider his masterpiece, *Nineteen Eighty-Four*, in 1949. In the same year, he remarried but died a few months later, on 21 January 1950 of tuberculosis.

Original contribution by Kathrin Auer

scholarship money provided by an institution to pay for sb.'s education
Eton Eton College, a famous independent school

embarrassment *Verlegenheit, Peinlichkeit*

colonialism the (former) practice of a powerful (usually European) country controlling another country
imperialism the idea of a powerful country influencing or controlling other countries
Hertfordshire county in southern England

class divide *Klassenschranke*

tuberculosis serious lung disease; *Tuberkulose*

Historical background

There was not one Russian Revolution but rather a series of movements for political liberation during the 19th century. The last revolution took place in November 1917 and ended the oppressive rule of the tsars that Russia had suffered under for hundreds of years. It brought power to the Bolsheviks, a revolutionary party committed to the ideas of Karl Marx. They believed that the working classes would eventually free themselves from the political and economic control of the ruling upper classes. Once this ultimate goal was achieved, a genuinely equal, socialist society would be established.

The Bolsheviks were led by Vladimir Lenin, who declared “All power to the Soviets” and promised “Peace, Land and Bread” to the masses.

The Bolsheviks had a highly effective propaganda campaign that told the people that living conditions would improve and wealth would be distributed more fairly.

After Lenin’s death in 1924 Leon Trotsky, Lenin’s former partner and second in command, and Joseph Stalin, the secretary of the Communist Party, fought to become his successor. Both had different ideas about the Soviet Union’s future. Trotsky planned to encourage world revolution, whereas Stalin believed Russia had to establish its power before attempting to spread revolution. Stalin became party leader, while Trotsky was exiled and then murdered in 1941. He was not the only one Stalin got rid off. During the 1930s Stalin ordered massive purges to eliminate anyone he considered a threat or suspected of disloyalty. Many of his political enemies or critics, and eventually even ordinary people, were murdered or sent to prison camps. Historical documents such as photographs and books were altered to eliminate the memory of the victims.

The Christian Church and the Muslim religion were forbidden, ethnic groups were persecuted and Russification was enforced.

Stalin had to be praised and applauded, newspapers celebrated him, poets wrote about him. His picture was everywhere and parents taught their children to love Stalin more than anyone else. Nobody dared to oppose him in any way for fear of being arrested.

Stalin’s aim was establishing rapid economic and industrial growth. However, by the end of the 1920s it had become obvious that this growth was not well planned. Russian agriculture was not producing enough to feed the population. People suffered from several famines and Stalin thus made collectivization compulsory. Some peasants were so opposed to the idea, they burned

liberation the process of freeing a country
oppressive tyrannical
tsar the former emperor of Russia

committed to bound to follow

eventually in the end

ultimate final and most important
genuinely truly

successor person that comes after sb.

purge the act of removing or often killing people because of their opposing views

to persecute to harass, to treat unfairly; *verfolgen*

collectivization joining private farms and putting them under the control of the state their crops and killed their animals before handing the farms over to the state. Still, by 1939, almost all of the land had been collectivized.

The improvements in production between 1928 and 1937 were phenomenal. Yet, the price for this was paid by the workers, many of whom were slave workers from the gulag. Work and living conditions were horrible and many died from accidents, starvation or cold.

Original contribution by Kathrin Auer

gulag Russian labour camps, mostly in Siberia

What is communism?

What communists believed:

1. The ideas of Karl Marx.
2. People should contribute to the public wealth according to their ability, but receive according to their needs.
3. The means of production should be owned equally by the whole community (hence communism), not as in capitalism where individuals (who might be very rich) own the means of production and leave the rest of society to be poor and oppressed wage slaves.
4. A deterministic interpretation of history, which said that society must inevitably develop through successive stages of slavery, feudalism, then capitalism, ending up with the violent overthrow of capitalism and the establishment of a communist society.
5. They should work to overthrow capitalism throughout the world by means of a revolution by the proletariat (workers).
6. Class was a feature of capitalist society, and should be destroyed and replaced by a society of equals.
7. The economy should be planned – controlled by the government.
8. Lenin changed Marx's ideas to add that a communist government first had to be a dictatorship, which was essential in order to bring in the communist state safely.

https://www.bbc.co.uk/bitesize/guides/zp8wcwx/revision/2 [08.08.2020]

inevitable cannot be prevented

feudalism *Feudalismus, mittelalterliche Lehnsherrschaft*

Aesop

The Dog, the Cock & the Fox

Aesop was a Greek storyteller who lived 620 – 564 BC. Although we have hardly any knowledge of his life – even his ethnicity remains unclear – and no writings by him have survived, he is thought to be the author of many fables now known as *Aesop's Fables*. Many of these tales are of animals that show very human characteristics, such as speaking and solving problems.

A Dog and a Cock, who were the best of friends, wished very much to see something of the world. So they decided to leave the farmyard and to set out into the world along the road that led to the woods. The two comrades travelled along in the very best of spirits and without meeting any adventure to speak of.

At nightfall the Cock, looking for a place to roost, as was his custom, spied nearby a hollow tree that he thought would do very nicely for a night's lodging. The Dog could creep inside and the Cock would fly up on one of the branches. So said, so done, and both slept very comfortably.

With the first glimmer of dawn the Cock awoke. For the moment he forgot just where he was. He thought he was still in the farmyard where it had been his duty to arouse the household at daybreak. So standing on tip-toes he flapped his wings and crowed lustily. But instead of awakening the farmer, he awakened a Fox not far off in the wood. The Fox immediately had rosy visions of a very delicious breakfast. Hurrying to the tree where the Cock was roosting, he said very politely:

"A hearty welcome to our woods, honoured sir. I cannot tell you how glad I am to see you here. I am quite sure we shall become the closest of friends."

"I feel highly flattered, kind sir," replied the Cock slyly. "If you will please go around to the door of my house at the foot of the tree, my porter will let you in."

The hungry but unsuspecting Fox, went around the tree as he was told, and in a twinkling the Dog had seized him.

Those who try to deceive may expect to be paid in their own coin.

http://read.gov/aesop/035.html [07.10.2020]

to roost (of birds) to sleep or rest

lodging accommodation

porter doorman

twinkling short moment

to deceive *betrügen*

Vladimir Lenin

How the Working People Can Be Saved from the Oppression of the Landowners and Capitalists For Ever

peasant farmer who owns or rents a small piece of land
to compel to force

to intimidate *einschüchtern*
to deceive to mislead by telling lies

tsarist supporter of the Russian tsar

unprecedented never known before
lash *Peitschenschlag*

yoke rough treatment; *Joch*

invincible too strong to be defeated

At the end of March 1919, Vladimir Lenin gave the following speech. It was translated by George Hannah.

The enemies of the working people, the landowners and capitalists say that the workers and peasants cannot live without them. "If it were not for us," they say, "there would be nobody to maintain order, to give out work, and to compel people to work. If it were not for us everything would collapse, and the state would fall to pieces. We have been driven away, but chaos will bring us back again." But this sort of talk by the landowners and capitalists will not confuse, intimidate, or deceive the workers and peasants. An army needs the strictest discipline; nevertheless, the class-conscious workers succeeded in uniting the peasants, succeeded in taking the old tsarist officers into their service, succeeded in building a victorious army.
The Red Army established unprecedentedly firm discipline – not by means of the lash, but based on the intelligence, loyalty and devotion of the workers and peasants themselves.
And so, to save the working people from the yoke of the landowners and capitalists for ever, to save them from the restoration of their power, it is necessary to build up a great Red Army of Labour. That army will be invincible if it is cemented by labour discipline. The workers and peasants must and will prove that they can properly distribute labour, establish devoted discipline and ensure loyalty in working for the common good, and can do it themselves, without the landowners and in spite of them, without the capitalists and in spite of them.
Labour discipline, enthusiasm for work, readiness for self-sacrifice, close alliance between the peasants and the workers – this is what will save the working people from the oppression of the landowners and capitalists for ever.

https://www.marxists.org/archive/lenin/works/1919/mar/x09.htm [01.02.2021]

Jonathan Russo

'Animal Farm' Perfectly Describes Life in the Era of Donald Trump

George Orwell's allegorical tale predicts Sean Spicer and fake news

Following President Donald Trump's inauguration, the Left's must-read book was George Orwell's 1984. Published in 1949, the dystopian novel predicts a world of authoritarian thought control, and it shot to the top of Amazon's bestseller list. This summer, a *1984* play from London is opening on Broadway. [...] There have been countless media references to the novel. [...] Margaret Atwood's *The Handmaid's Tale* is also getting a second wind. In her 1985 book, the powerful have reduced fertile women to reproductive slaves for the elite's infertile wives. Already released as a film [...] the book has now reappeared as a miniseries [...]. Part of the marketing plan is to make the story an allegory to the Trump administration. Almost everyone is having fun with the comparison.

But these are the wrong books to read and shows to watch. A much more relevant work is Orwell's 1945 novella *Animal Farm.* As in *1984,* he imagines a harsh political landscape. Yet, *Animal Farm* is much subtler – and more powerful – than *1984* or the improbable *Handmaid's Tale.*

There is no sign that there is or will be any effective thought control or political repression as described in *1984*. Democracy seems as powerful as ever. [...]

Animal Farm envisioned a somewhat different scenario for political promises. Writing about the Russian Revolution's failures, Orwell imagined a farm that overthrew its human master and replaced him with a collective leadership of pigs. These clever pigs promised to reorganize society along egalitarian (populist) lines with the animal workers being rewarded for their labor on a just and fair farm. Mirroring Russia, where Stalin replaced Trotsky and Lenin's vision with the Gulag camps and a system of brutal repression and corruption, the ruling pigs of *Animal Farm* gradually became human-like and their promises of change forgotten.

The leaders of *Animal Farm* maintained thought control by obscuring the facts with smokescreens. In this way, the allegory to the Trump administration is dead on. Executives from Wall Street, once lambasted by Trump as "get[ting] away with murder," are now in charge. The "currency manipulator" to be punished on Trump's first day in office, China, is now a strategic ally helping to fend off North Korea.

to predict to see into the future
Sean Spicer was White House Press Secretary and Communications Director under President Trump in 2017

fertile *here*: able to have children

improbable unlikely

Gulag camps system of labour camps, mostly in Siberia
repression *Unterdrückung*

to obscure to make it difficult to hear, see or understand
smokescreen *Verschleierung*
dead on (*infml.*) completely right
to lambast to attack
currency *Währung*

to fend off to defend against

habitué (*fml.*) regular visitor

unprecedented never happened before

donation *Spende*

governance activity of governing a country

to placate [plə'keɪt] to calm

"drain the swamp" refers to Trump's plan to fix the problems of Washington and the federal government

threat [θret] *Drohung*

to squabble to argue noisily

spin *Verdrehung*

to erase to delete, to remove

to recall to remember

to alter to change

spokespig (made up word) spokesperson

to reconcile to make opposing ideas agree and co-exist

to parse to separate

non sequitur (*fml.*) a statement that does not logically follow what has previously been said

guidepost *Wegweiser*

Trump's transformation into a golf course habitué after roundly criticizing his predecessor's golf outings is right out of *Animal Farm.* [...]

That the populist Trump has offered unprecedented access to some of the largest corporations in America in exchange for their millions of dollars of donations is another page straight out of *Animal Farm.* The entire façade of governance in *Animal Farm* was meant to placate the horses, sheep and chickens with feel-good slogans and false agendas. Trump's "drain the swamp" mantra would have been an appropriate *Animal Farm* infrastructure slogan. The pigs, who were afraid they would lose control of the farm, created imaginary threats as a tactic to bind their subjects. How is this different from Trump's alerting us to the threat of Mexican rapists?

Orwell, who had perhaps the most brilliant political mind of the twentieth century, even anticipated the phenomenon of fake news. The historic Battle of the Cowshed, in which the animals liberated the farm from the humans, was told and retold with fake news added as the pigs began to squabble. New spins on the facts were constantly required. Thus, a true hero of the Battle of the Cowshed, Snowball, was later reported to have sided with the humans. Even Trump's deleted tweet about how it was an "honor to host [Palestinian] President Mahmoud Abbas" at the White House was foreseen in *Animal Farm*, as writing on the barn wall was changed and erased as politically necessary. The animals could not recall the original writings or how they were altered.

Orwell even anticipated Sean Spicer. The pigs have a spokespig named Squealer who is in charge of reconciling the irreconcilable and parsing the absurdities of non sequitur pronouncements from the pigs' administration. To read Squealer's spin on the changes in farm policy is a literary treat no reader will ever forget.

So, if you are looking for allegorical literature to understand today's politics, *Animal Farm* is a great guidepost. It is much more politically relevant than *1984* or *Handmaid's Tale.* It should be the next book to jump to the top of Amazon's bestseller list. Do yourself a favor and secure a copy fast.

https://observer.com/2017/05/donald-trump-george-orwell-animal-farm, 09.05.2017 [21.08.2020].

Finn Mayer-Kuckuck

Selbst Grimassen werden zensiert

Beim nationalen Volkskongress der Kommunistischen Partei Chinas sind zustimmende Blicke gefragt; ein Augenrollen wurde im Netz gelöscht.

Augenrollen eye-roll

Ein Augenrollen sagt mehr als Tausend Worte. In diesem Fall hat Liang Xiangyi, eine Journalistin des Internetportals Yicai.com, mit ihrer Mimik das ausgedrückt, was alle im Raum dachten: Wie langweilig! Der Auslöser dieser Reaktion war die Frage einer anderen Journalistin – einer Dame in einem roten Blazer von einem staatlichen TV-Sender für Chinesen in Übersee. Die Dame hatte auf einer Pressekonferenz am Rande des Volkskongresses in Peking eine jener „Fragen“ gestellt, die vor allem aus umfangreichem Lob für die Regierung bestehen.

Volkskongress National People's Congress; highest organ of state power of the People's Republic of China

Liang ist jetzt in China berühmt – doch das Video von diesem kostbaren Moment ist zensiert. Das Augenrollen war live im Fernsehen zu sehen und verbreitete sich als Video-Schnipsel sofort in den sozialen Medien. Die Internetnutzer finden ihn erfrischend. „Dieser Blick wird das einzige sein, an das ich mich von diesem Volkskongress erinnere“, schrieb ein Blogger. Die Staatsmedien übertragen jede Propagandarede mit all ihren Phrasen in Länge und Breite. Wem da nicht langweilig wird, der muss schon ein sehr linientreuer Kommunist sein. Selbst Mitglieder des Zentralkomitees der Partei nicken auf dem Volkskongress zuweilen ein. […]

Staatsmedien state media
Propagandarede propaganda speech
linientreu loyal to the party line, lineal
Zentralkomitte Central Committe (of a communist party)

Präsident Xi Jinping und seine Politik, die Macht der Partei, der Reichtum der Genossen an der Spitze, Taiwan als Teil Chinas, das Massaker von 1989 – da greifen die Überwacher ein. Journalistin Liang hatte die unsichtbare Grenze nun durch das Augenrollen überschritten: Das Video ließ sich auf den beliebtesten Plattformen nicht mehr öffentlich posten. Die Nutzer der weit verbreiteten App „Wechat“ konnten es sich am Mittwoch zwar einander noch direkt zuschicken, aber zum Teil nicht mehr in Gruppenunterhaltungen einstellen. Der derzeit laufende Volkskongress hat bereits eine Reihe von originellen Zensurentscheidungen hervorgebracht. Fotos von Pu dem Bären – und seine Erwähnung auf Chinesisch – waren beispielsweise strikt verboten. „Pu“ steht für Xi, seit Internetnutzer eine verblüffende Ähnlichkeit des Bären mit dem Staatschef festgestellt haben.

Pu der Bär Winnie-the-Pooh, fictional teddy bear created by the English author A.A. Milne and illustrator E. H. Shepard

Es stimmt zwar nicht, dass „der Buchstabe N im Netz gesperrt“ sei, wie einige Medien berichteten. (Wie auch?) Doch der Suchbegriff „Xi Zedong“ ergibt bei der führenden Suchmaschine Baidu „keine Treffer“. Dabei handelt es sich um eine Mischung

Mao Zedong (1893 - 1976) founder of the People's Republic of China
Suchmaschinen search engine
verkommen to decay
Inhaltsaufsicht content supervision
privatwirtschaftlich commercial
Unternehmensbeteiligung shareholding
Staatsvermögen national assets
Staatsrat State Council, privy council
staatseigen state-owned
Überseeinvestition overseas investment
Anlagerisiko investment risk

der Namen des derzeitigen Präsidenten mit dem des Ex-Diktators Mao Zedong. Staatlich unabhängige Suchmaschinen wie Google sind in China gesperrt; Microsoft Bing allerdings macht die Zensur in vollem Umfang mit. [...]

Auch Hinweise auf George Orwells Fabel „Farm der Tiere" verschwanden in diesen Tagen massenhaft aus dem Netz. Orwell beschreibt darin, wie der Sozialismus zu einer Gewaltherrschaft verkommt, in der die ehemaligen Anführer der Revolution sich zur neuen Aristokratie machen.

In allen Internetfirmen sitzen in den Abteilungen für Inhaltsaufsicht seit 2015 besonders ausgebildete Polizisten neben den regulären Mitarbeitern. Es ist zwar die Pflicht von Anbietern wie Tencent und Sina, ihre Seiten politisch sauber zu halten und sie beschäftigen dafür jeweils Tausende von Mitarbeitern rund um die Uhr. Doch die privatwirtschaftlichen Zensoren stimmen sich auch laufend mit den staatlichen Zensurbehörden ab. Immer ausgefeiltere Computerprogramme unterstützen die Aufseher bei ihrer Arbeit und machen sie auf potenziell mehrdeutige Inhalte aufmerksam. Jetzt war es also ein Augenrollen. Die genervte Journalistin Liang erfährt dabei von allen Seiten Zustimmung.

Kein Wunder, schließlich lautete die Frage der linientreuen Kollegin neben ihr: „Die Umgestaltung der Verantwortlichkeitsstruktur für die Aufsicht über staatliche Unternehmensbeteiligungen ist eine Frage von großem Interesse für das chinesische Volk. Welche Neuerungen planen Sie als Direktor der Kommission zur Kontrolle und Verwaltung von Staatsvermögen unter dem Staatsrat im Jahr 2018? In diesem Jahr feiern wir den 40. Jahrestag der Reform- und Öffnungspolitik, und unser Land tritt in eine neue Phase der Offenheit gegenüber der Welt ein. Die Kommunistische Partei unter Generalsekretär Xi Jinping treibt die Initiative Ein-Gürtel-Eine-Straße weiter voran, daher haben staatseigene Betriebe ihre Investitionen entlang der Seidenstraße erhöht. Wie können die Überseeinvestitionen der Staatsbetriebe so verwaltet werden, dass keine Anlagerisiken auftreten? Welche Mechanismen wurden bisher eingeführt, und was sind die Ergebnisse der Überwachung?"

Das Augenrollen erfolgte bereits während des ersten Drittels dieser Frage. Die Journalistin im roten Blazer hat derweil in ihrem Beitrag alle Schlagworte eingefügt, die derzeit von der Zensurbehörde erwünscht sind: Seidenstraße, Reform, Öffnung, die Führung durch Xi und Auslandsinvestitionen. Was jetzt aus Liangs eigener Karriere wird, ist offen.

https://www.fr.de/politik/selbst-grimassen-werden-zensiert-10994372.html, 14.03.2018 [08.08.2020]

Skills & vocabulary

Allegories, fables and parables

An **allegory** is a fictional narrative in which the characters and events are symbols of something else. Its metaphorical meaning usually has moral, political, social or religious significance while the characters are personifications of abstract ideas like pride, wisdom or loyalty. Hence, allegorical stories always have a literal and a symbolic meaning.

Fables are a form of allegory. They are shorter stories, in which animals act like humans or represent human traits. Usually they are didactic, they want to teach a certain moral lesson, comment on something or shine light on something that is generally accepted as right. Sometimes, they use satire in their criticism. This means that humour and ridicule are employed to deride something. The fable's moral may be obvious from the text or explained at the end of the story. Fables can be written in prose or in verse.

Parables are another form of allegory. The main difference between parables and fables is that the first does not employ animals but humans.

didactic designed to teach sth.

ridicule mockery; *Verspottung*
to deride sth./sb. to belittle sb./sth.
prose text that is not poetry
verse poetry

How to analyse a (political) speech

Speeches, and political speeches in particular, are non-fictional texts that try to convince their recipients of something. They are called persuasive texts and use stylistic devices, including imperatives, to appeal to their audience. Therefore, when dealing with speeches, you should always start by asking:

- Who is the speaker?
- Who is the recipient?
- What are the speaker's intentions?
- What is the context, i. e. where and when is the speech delivered?

recipient who a message is meant for, addressee

Structure and language

The effectiveness of a speech will be determined by the quality of an author's **arguments and their arrangement** and the author's use of language.

Most of the time, the first thing a speaker will do is to try to win the audience's attention, e.g. with **a humorous anecdote or remark,** as President Obama did during his speech at the 2016 White House Correspondents' Dinner.

> (After using a song going
> "You're gonna miss me when I'm
> gone" for his entrance)
> You can't say it, but you know it's true.
> *Barack Obama, 2016*

Alternatively, the speaker may want to show the audience the importance of their speech with **a serious remark** like President Bush did on the evening of 9/11 in 2001.

deliberate planned and intentional

> Good evening. Today, our fellow
> citizens, our way of life, our very
> freedom came under attack in a series
> of deliberate and deadly terrorist acts.
> *George W. Bush, 2001*

to secure to obtain
to pursue to follow, to continue

cohesive forming a united whole

After having secured the audience's interest, the goal of the speech needs to be pursued, which is best done by presenting the speaker's ideas and arguments in a cohesive manner. Often, political speeches will ask their listeners for their trust (and hence votes) or call them to action.

Connecting with the audience

Not only is it important to convince the audience with well thought-out arguments and an easy-to-follow structure. It is also vital to interact and connect with the audience on an emotional level.

- One frequently used way of achieving this is by using the **personal pronouns** 'I', 'you' and 'we' to create a personal relationship and establish some sort of group feeling.

humbled overwhelmed

sacrifice *Opfer*
to bestow to give

> My fellow citizens: I stand here
> today humbled by the task before us,
> grateful for the trust you have bestowed,
> mindful to the sacrifices borne by our
> ancestors.
> *Barack Obama, 2009*

- If something is painful and hard, the speaker should acknowledge this and be open about it.

> And let me begin by acknowledging that, although all of us have been feeling pain, uncertainty, disruption, some folks have been feeling it more than others.
> *Barack Obama, 2020*

disruption sth. that interrupts sb.'s normal life

- **Emotive language** will also help establish an emotional relationship as it will help the audience understand the speaker's feelings. So, instead of simply using the term 'victims', President Bush further described those who died in the 9/11 attacks as parents and friends.

emotive causing people to feel strong emotions

> The victims were in airplanes, or in their offices; secretaries, businessmen and women, military and federal workers; moms and dads, friends and neighbors.
> *George W. Bush, 2001*

- Similarly, the speaker may want to **address certain groups** in the audience (e.g. single parents, ethnic minorities, etc.) to make them feel more included and seen.
- **Rhetorical questions**, i.e. questions that the speaker does not expect an answer to, as the answer is already implied in the question, are yet another way to connect with the audience.
- A speaker may be '**fishing for compliments**', i.e. presenting himself or herself in inferior terms.

Rhetorical devices in speeches

Rhetorical devices are fairly common in speeches as they make language more vivid and help illustrate the speaker's intentions.

- **Metaphors** and **similes** are stylistic devices that compare things or ideas explicitly or implicitly.

> One hundred years later, the Negro
> lives on a lonely island of poverty
> in the midst of a vast ocean of
> material prosperity.
> *Martin Luther King, 1963*

- **Allusion**, **hyperbole** [haɪ'pɜ:(r)bəli], i.e. exaggeration, and litotes, i.e. the opposites, also add to the audience's attention.
- **Antithesis** or **contrast** can help simplify more complex issues. Complex issues can also be simplified by presenting only two sides.

> Either you are with us or you are
> with the terrorists.
> *George W. Bush, 2001*

- When listening to a speech there is usually no way to rewind and listen to certain parts again. A good speaker will take this into account and employ **repetition** to make a lasting impression and to highlight the vital aspects.
  Different types of repetition include **anaphora** (repeating the same word or phrase at the beginning of each sentence), **parallelism** (repeating similar sentence structures) and **alliteration** (choosing words that begin with the same letter) but also **synonyms** (different words with the same meaning).

> We will plan carefully; we will act
> with the full power of the United
> States military; we will act with
> allies at our side, and we will prevail.
> *George W. Bush, 2002*

Vocabulary: Allegories, fables, parables and political speeches

allegories, fables, parables	
to address	*ansprechen*
allegory, allegorical	*Allegorie, allegorisch*
to appeal to	*appellieren an*
to apply sth. to sth.	*etw. auf etw. übertragen, anwenden*
behaviour, to behave	*Verhalten, sich verhalten*
character trait	*Charakterzug*
to concern	*betreffen*
denouement	*Ausgang, (Auf)Lösung*
didactic	*didaktisch, lehrend*
direct, explicit	*direkt*
ending	*Ende*
excess	*Auswuchs*
to exemplify	*exemplarisch darstellen*
to expose	*entblößen*
exposition	*Einleitung*
(animal) fable	*(Tier)Fabel*
fault, flaw	*Fehler*
fictional narrative	*fiktive Erzählung*
human beings, human	*Menschen, menschlich*
to illustrate	*illustrieren, verdeutlichen*
imaginary	*ausgedacht*
implicit	*implizit*
indirect	*indirekt*
interpretation, to interpret	*Interpretation, interpretieren*
introduction, to introduce	*Einführung, einführen*
ironic(al)	*ironisch*
literary meaning	*wörtliche Bedeutung*
main character	*Hauptfigur*
metaphor, metaphorical	*Metapher, metaphorisch*
moral	*Moral*
parable	*Parabel*
personification	*Personifizierung*

allegories, fables, parables	
prose	*Prosa*
protagonist	*Protagonist*
to represent	*repräsentieren, darstellen*
significance, to signify	*Bedeutung, bedeuten*
to stand for sth.	*für etwas stehen*
symbolic meaning	*symbolische Bedeutung*
tragic	*tragisch*
verse	*Dichtung*

political speeches	
according to	*nach*
to admit	*zugeben, einräumen*
anecdote	*Anekdote*
to appeal to	*appellieren an*
to attack	*angreifen*
attitude	*Einstellung*
audience	*Publikum*
to blame others for one's failures	*andere für die eigenen Fehler beschuldigen, verantwortlich machen*
catchphrase	*Schlagwort*
concise	*knapp, prägnant*
connected	*verknüpft*
to contest sth.	*etw. bestreiten*
to create a feeling of solidarity	*ein Solidaritätsgefühl schaffen*
to diminish	*abschwächen*
to distort facts	*Fakten verdrehen, verzerren*
effect	*Wirkung*
elevated speech level	*gehobenes Sprachniveau*
emotive	*gefühlsbetonend*
to exaggerate	*übertreiben*
expression	*Ausdruck*
frequent use	*häufige Verwendung*
full of clichés	*voller Klischees*
to get sb. to act, to mobilize sb. to take action	*jdn. zum Handeln bringen*

political speeches	
to give/make a speech on/ about	*eine Rede halten*
to give sth. publicity	*etw. bekannt machen*
ideology, ideological	*Ideologie, ideologisch*
imperative	*Imperativ, Befehlsform*
to impose one's opinion on the listeners	*den Zuhörern die eigene Meinung aufzwingen*
to influence	*beeinflussen*
juxtaposed	*(häufig Gegensätzliches) nebeneinander gestellt*
to launch into a polemic	*in Polemik verfallen*
to misrepresent sth.	*etw. falsch wiedergeben*
objective	*Ziel*
opponent; opposing	*Gegner; gegnerisch*
to point out one's own merits	*die eigenen Verdienste herausstellen*
positive/negative associations	*positive/negative Assoziationen*
to praise	*loben*
to recognize	*anerkennen*
remark	*Bemerkung*
to simplify facts	*Fakten vereinfachen*
speaker	*Redner*
to speak in public	*in der Öffentlichkeit reden*
to spread propaganda	*Propaganda verbreiten*
statement	*Aussage*
to state clearly	*klar aussagen/darstellen*
stereotypical	*stereotyp*
to support the interests of	*die Interessen von … unterstützen*
techniques of persuasion	*Überredungstechniken*
vague form of wording	*vage Formulierung*

Acknowledgements

|Alamy Stock Photo (RMB), Abingdon/Oxfordshire: GL Archive 76.1; public domain sourced/access rights from Historic Collection 72.1. |iStockphoto.com, Calgary: clu 75.1.